Sir Matt Busby w... mining village of .... began his lifelong association with soccer in 1929 as a member of the Manchester City team. He transferred to Liverpool and also became a Scottish International, captaining them through the war years. In 1945 he was appointed manager of Manchester United, a position he held until 1969 when he handed over team affairs to become general manager. In 1971 he joined United's board of directors. For his services to the game he was awarded the CBE in 1958 and was knighted in 1968; in 1972 he was made a Knight Commander of St Gregory and is a Freeman of the City of Manchester.

Soccer at the Top

My Life in Football

MATT BUSBY

SPHERE BOOKS LIMITED
30/32 Gray's Inn Road, London WC1X 8JL

First published in Great Britain by Weidenfeld and Nicolson Ltd 1973
Copyright © Beaverbrook Newspapers Ltd 1973
Published by Sphere Books 1974

To Jean

Grateful thanks to Bill Fryer, my long-standing friend, for
his considerable help in producing this book.

TRADE
MARK

Set in Linotype Times

Printed in Great Britain by
Hazell Watson & Viney Ltd
Aylesbury, Bucks

ISBN 0 7221 2096 6

CONTENTS

FOREWORD

I am sure that this book will be read by many in and outside Manchester to whom the name of Sir Matt Busby is so well known that a foreword is hardly necessary.

I first met Matt when he and I were 'performers' in the 1934 Cup Final at Wembley – he as a right-half of Manchester City, and I as the referee. Later, when I became secretary of the Football Association and he manager of United we met often, particularly as we were both keen to get English clubs into Europe and also because so many of his gifted players became internationals. Matt was also selected to be the manager of the first British team to compete in the Olympic Games after the four British Football Associations rejoined FIFA. The players were selected from each of the four British countries. It was no easy task to manage the team, especially as the number of officials from the four countries almost outnumbered the players and they – the members – formed a selection committee and wanted to pick the teams to represent Great Britain.

When war broke out in 1939 I was asked to recommend suitable sports players to join the Army and RAF Physical Training Staffs and Matt was soon a sergeant in the Army PE Corps stationed at the Army School of PT at Aldershot for training. During that period he played for Reading and in international matches at Wembley and Glasgow when matches were arranged for the Red Cross. Later he was posted to Italy and formed a team which included such players as Joe Mercer and Cliff Britton.

7

This book does not tell you what a great player Matt was. At right-half, with Bray at left-half, in the Manchester City side he played the ball on the ground and pushed a pass to an unmarked forward before defences could retreat. If only half-backs would do this today instead of carrying the ball where they ought quickly and accurately to send it, there would be fewer cries for reforms to increase the scoring rate.

Readers of this book will follow Matt's career as a manager. A born leader, a 'no nonsense' example to his players, no 'yes-man' to his employers. His army experiences had taught him that there can be only one officer commanding. He learnt how to delegate duties and expected subordinates to accept responsibility. He was a good 'picker', a good judge of character both of staff and players, and fortunately for Manchester United a good 'mixer'. It is refreshing and entertaining to read how he understood and managed the great players he 'inherited', such as Johnny Carey, Charlie Mitten, Allenby Chilton, Jack Rowley, Jack Crompton, Henry Cockburn and many others, all with different characters, different temperaments, and made them into a team which were Football League runners-up in 1947, 1948, 1949, 1951 and Champions in 1952.

I am sure that readers of this book will see emerging the image of a great man, because the account of his dealings with so many players and coaches is fascinating. His 'accord' with Jimmy Murphy and others are lessons to all managers, coaches and players. His foresight in planning the Manchester United 'nursery' from which sprang the Busby Babes was remarkable.

I was privileged to see many of the 'Babes' play in England XIs at different levels. Duncan Edwards was one who was outstanding. Had he lived, he would have been England's captain for years.

Many readers will recall the tragedy of Munich when they read Matt's memories of it. I was in Edinburgh attending meetings when Ernest Miller, my assistant at the Football Association, telephoned me at 5 p.m. to tell me of the disaster. I left on the first plane to London, unable to do anything except mourn those friends whom I had known so well, the players and journalists including Frank Swift and Archie Ledbrooke.

The chapters on how Matt 'filled the gap' are exciting, especially as they lead to the winning of the FA Cup trophy. When he was awarded the CBE I was asked by an official at Buckingham Palace whether Matt would like Her Majesty to decorate him with it at Wembley on the occasion of the Final. I said I thought the atmosphere would be already tense and excitable and that Matt would prefer to to go with his wife and members of his family to a normal investiture at Buckingham Palace.

The views which Matt expresses about directors, managers, players, including George Best, legislators and 'backroom boys', the advice he gave to many of them and the manner in which he dealt with them in his office, on and off the field, will give many hours of enjoyable reading to his friends and fans. It is a record of his life's work from boyhood to the elevated positions he fills to date. Truly 'This is his life'.

I have much pleasure in recommending this book and hope it will give enjoyment to thousands of followers of football who know and respect the name of Sir Matt Busby.

May 1973   *STANLEY ROUS*

PART ONE

IN MY WAY

THE YOUNG DICTATOR

37 Craigwell Road,
Prestwich,
Manchester.
15 December 1944.

Dear Matt,

No doubt you will be surprised to get this letter from your old pal Louis. Well Matt I have been trying for the past month to find you and not having your Reg. address I could not trust a letter going to Liverpool, as what I have to say is so important. I don't know if you have considered about what you are going to do when the war is over, but I have a great job for you if you are willing to take it on. Will you get into touch with me at the above address and when you do I can explain things to you better, when I know there will be no danger of interception. Now Matt I hope this is plain to you. You see I have not forgotten my old friend either in my prayers or in your future welfare. I hope your good wife and family are well and please God you will soon be home to join their happy circle.

Wishing you a very Happy Xmas and a lucky New Year. Wilth all God's Blessings in you and yours.

Your Old Pal
Louis Rocca.

The late Louis Rocca was Manchester United's chief scout, at a time when scouting was not the highly organized network it is now. He was one of the most respected judges of footballers in the land. But he did not count only on his judgement. He had contacts wherever the game was played.

The measure of the man was that while he seemed to know every other good judge in the game all of these and lesser judges knew Louis Rocca. And it was fairly certain that if a player *was* a player, in the Football League or out of it, Louis Rocca knew about him.

Call it confidence, conceit, arrogance, or ignorance, but I was unequivocal about it. At the advanced age of thirty-five I would accept the managership of Manchester United only if they would let me have all my own way. As the manager I would want to manage. I would be the boss.

This being so I would not have any excuse if I failed. Nor would I offer any. They could kick me out.

The manager who is also the boss of a football club in the 1970s may have become commonplace. I hope he is. But he is not universal. And in 1945 he was unheard of. In those days the manager had the title and usually everybody else made the decisions. Directors chipped in with their ideas of picking a team, and niggled when, umpteen people having poked their noses and opinions in, a team emerged and inevitably differed from their several choices.

Secretaries were others who were apt to do more managing than the managers. Only a few would criticize secretaries as a race. An efficient secretary knows nearly all. But he must not be a know-all. He is the adjutant, not the commanding officer.

I have never joined in the popular game of belittling football club directors simply *because* they are football club directors. I have always said, look at the top when analysing clubs who have lasting success and there you will find the original cause of the happy effect. There was never a club with an unhappy chairman and an unhappy board that achieved lasting success at anything.

Directors appoint a manager to manage. Some still do not allow them to do so. When will they ever learn?

But what right had I, what qualification had I to demand virtual dictatorship of a famous football club? My early background, which I propose to skim over since I have written about it before, would not seem to have qualified me for such a task. I, a pit boy from Bellshill, near Glasgow, who had lost his father in the First World War and who, because of the necessity to help mother's family budget, had not been able to follow the headmaster's advice

13

and train for school-teaching. Nor had I ever managed a football club, and, indeed, I could have played on for another year or two with Liverpool and then perhaps taken a staff job there.

But I *did* think I knew about football and footballers. Technical knowledge alone will not make a manager in any organization. It is incomplete without a feeling for people. Whether the loss of my father had subconsciously given me a feeling of being unprotected, I do not know. Certainly there is some gap for a boy without a father when all other boys around him could talk about theirs incessantly and did.

Perhaps it induced in me some paternal, protective feeling for other unfortunate or sensitive young people. Whatever induced it I had it. I was only a boy when I left home for the first time to go to Manchester City. Not all boys are tough and adventurous, though in the Seventies fledglings seem to regard it as 'chicken' *not* to leave the nest, whereas it was only the rare bird who flew before the war.

Anyway I was homesick, and it did not help when, having used a senior player's football boots by mistake one day, he gave me a tremendous blasting.

There was a seemingly unbridgeable gulf between first team players and the rest, and an even wider gulf between players and management. They were office managers in those days. A player saw the manager only on Saturday in the coach or if he called you up to his office for a rocket.

I was appalled about those gulfs and about the indignities that were heaped on players. There are players, of course, who are too thick to understand that they are being got at. There are others who feel every stinging, sarcastic thrust, every bullying, scoffing, snide wisecrack.

Perhaps my background had made me a little older than my years, but, long before I became established, long before I was captain of Scotland, long before I moved from Manchester City to Liverpool, I vowed that if ever I became a manager I would respect players as individuals who needed individual treatment and thereby try to inspire respect from them.

On top of this, in the war so recently ended I had 'managed' or, as the Army would put it, been 'i/c' the Army football team. All the players in this team were in the top class of the game. And I quickly realized the importance of dele-

14

gation. For example, one of the team was Joe Mercer, who knew something about provisions from his wife's family's grocery business. I made Joe 'i/c Rations'. We ate well.

Joe, of course, was the Everton and England (and later Arsenal) wing-half. And I created jobs for two more Everton and England players, Tommy Lawton and Cliff Britton, and a Manchester City (and later England) goalkeeper called Frank Swift.

Tommy and Frank had 'borrowed' our Army truck to make a trip to Pompeii, so I thought I had better keep firmer control on the vehicle and I thereupon appointed Cliff 'i/c Transport'. Tommy and Frank I gave the job of baggage men. Great men all, but very happy to fulfil these vital tasks for me.

But now I was out of the Army and approaching the end of my playing career. And here was a big job beckoning.

I had no doubt about my technical knowledge. Professional footballers are apt to be very confident about these things. I had experience of being 'in charge' of top-class players. Most of all I had my theories about the psychology needed for management, footballer-management, the essential qualities I felt had been missing in the game as I had known it.

The gulfs must go, I knew, and I felt that this could only happen by putting myself into a position in which my respect for directors would draw *them* closer to me, paradoxically without their interfering, and the same with the secretary and the rest of the staff, and by dealing with each player as an individual, even to the extent of stressing that it was important for him to *be* an individual. As long as he behaved himself, that is.

Everybody is important to himself – the director, the manager, the secretary, the players, the trainers, the coaches, the groundsman, the tea ladies, the lot. Their importance must not only be appreciated. It must be *seen* to be appreciated.

I had decided years before that bullying could at best bring only instant obedience and never lasting results. I had decided that loud noises were not my forte, and that strength was not measured in decibels.

Manchester had other attractions beside Manchester United's managership. My wife, Jean, and I loved Manchester. Our closest friends were there. We still love Manchester, our home for most of our lives.

And there was the salary – £750 per annum.

For my cheek I got the job. My way, for better or for worse.

I took a bus to the Cornbrook Cold Storage. Not many footballers had motor cars in 1945, especially footballers who had recently been demobilized from the Services. The Cornbrook Cold Storage was one of the business interests of Mr Jimmy Gibson, the Manchester United chairman. One of its small offices housed the entire Manchester United administration staff, comprising Walter Crickmer, the club secretary, his assistant, who was a youth called Leslie Olive, a typist borrowed from Cornbrook Cold Storage, and now – me. It was about a mile from the bomb-wrecked United ground.

There we conducted the business of rebuilding Manchester United, a team with no ground and no money. There, too, were conducted the club's board meetings.

To get among the players as they trained required me to take two buses, one to Town and one from Town to The Cliff, Lower Broughton, three or four miles away. The Cliff, now a magnificent establishment for the preparation of footballers, is still United's training HQ. Tuesday and Thursday evenings were the training period, except for those who could train in the daytime, the few who were already demobbed for example. Motor cars and coaches have diminished that three or four miles journey from an hour to a few minutes. We had not been spoiled by the motor car then. We walked or took a bus. I doubt that either harmed us much.

In that small office there was not much room for dreaming, or much time. But dream I did.

THE 'NO' MAN

I was manager of Manchester United, a very raw young manager. I sat in the directors' box and a director sat behind me. During the game he leaned forward and said in a voice that people around him could hear: 'Why didn't you do so-and-so?'

'Shall I turn round and give him a blast?' I asked myself. But my judgement said: 'No. Wait.' I waited for the first convenient moment. Convenient? It was in the 'gents'. I said to him: 'Never dare to say anything like that to me when other people can hear you.' And I put it on the agenda for the next board meeting: 'Interference by directors'.

In my first full Football League season (1946-7), the first season after the war, we finished runners-up in the First Division to Liverpool. We played our home games at Manchester City's Maine Road ground, of course, Old Trafford being still under repair from the ravages of the war. (In fact we went back 'home' for the beginning of season 1949-50.)

In the season 1947-8, we ran into an indifferent spell and were around sixteenth in the table. I was still a bit raw.

Mr Jimmy Gibson, the chairman, who had financed and saved the club in 1931, was something of an autocrat. Everybody stood to attention when he approached. One of the first things he had said to me when I took the job was: 'I hope you are not going to spend a lot of money.'

His great love for Manchester United exceeded his technical knowledge of the game. But he was anxious, no, determined, to do something about our lean spell. He wanted me to sign somebody – *anybody* I think. As soon as he saw in a newspaper that a player was 'on offer' I could be sure he would be along that morning to ask if I was about to buy him. The answer had always been 'No', because I had decided each time that the player was not the one I required.

But we *were* needing a player, and, one day, to use the words of another dictator, Mr Gibson's patience was exhausted. A Newcastle United player had been transfer-listed. Mr Gibson, as usual, asked me was I going to sign him. I said: 'No, he is not good for us.'

This was too much for the chairman. 'You are always telling me "No",' he said, and before I had time to explain why, he went on: 'Well I'm telling *you* now. Go and sign him' – the obvious implication being: 'Or else!'

'No,' I said, 'and I will remind you of two things, Mr Gibson. I am here to manage the club and part of management is giving you advice. And the second is that I lived long before I ever saw you.'

17

I thought he was about to have a fit. He brandished his stick in the air until I thought he would hit me with it. But instead he stamped out of the room.

It looked as though I had overdone my independence line. But I had decided that although I would take advice I would still insist on making my own decisions. I would stand on my own feet. If not, my judgement said, I would find myself doing things other people's way. How could I be judged or even judge myself if my decisions were made for me?

About fifteen minutes later he came back and said: 'Mr Busby, you are a very strong-minded person.' I said: '*You* are a very strong-minded person.' And he said: 'Well I have come back and I want to say I am sorry this has happened. We will carry on as we were.'

From that day he neither interfered with my decisions nor brooked any interference with them by anyone else. At a board meeting he would say: 'Mr Busby says this.' And whatever I had said, 'this' would be that, and no argument. Our respect for each other was complete.

Later, when he was a sick man confined to his bed, Jimmy Gibson used to send for me and say: 'Anybody interfering with you, Mr Busby? If there is he will have to go.'

We finished that second season runners-up in the First Division again, and winners of the FA Cup. Sadly, Mr Gibson was too ill to go to Wembley. But he knew things had indeed worked out.

In my early days as manager, Harold Hardman, who was later to become the second of only three chairmen United have had in my time, could be a difficult old man. He had been a player, of course, and even this can have its snags. He was an old man with old-fashioned and inflexible ideas, which is a fault with some older directors. Today's young people should remember that the generation gap is not a 1970s invention.

But Harold Hardman and I got to know each other, and another excellent relationship began and lasted. He would say at the board meeting: 'Our manager has asked us for advice and we will give it to him (pause) and then he'll please his bloody self.'

I even had to referee sometimes in those early days. Some directors would argue for hours about some small point, usually because two of them, for instance, would simply not agree about anything. If one said black the other said white. Never have I seen a more contrary pair. They both wanted the best for the club, but they could never agree about anything, particularly policy matters. The argument might become so bitter that I would have to keep them apart physically.

One of the bones of contention between the two at the time was the rebuilding of the stand at Old Trafford. Bill Petherbridge, the more cautious, wanted us to take what compensation we got and rebuild it as it was, the cheaper way, which, since we had no money to spare, was logical enough. Dr McLean, more futuristic, wanted some bolder, more modern approach, which, I suppose, since we all had ambitions for the club, was also logical. But the argument would become hotter and hotter until, like a boxing referee, I had to step in and say: 'Break.'

When I had been manager for about eighteen months, the chairman of another club offered me its management. I said: 'You have a manager,' but he pooh-poohed that, so I said: 'I am under contract,' and he said: 'Contracts are made to be broken,' and I said: 'Not mine.'

I heard later that when this same chairman asked his manager to show him the team he had picked he would take the sheet from the manager's hand and tear it up and say: 'Now, we'll pick a team.'

It could be imagined what sort of a time he and I would have had if I had taken his offer. Imagine, too, how much store I could have set by any contract I signed with him. He did not sign a manager to manage. He wanted someone to bully.

I have no doubt that I learned from Jimmy Gibson and Harold Hardman and I like to think that I educated them in the matter of football management.

I certainly learned from Walter Crickmer, the secretary, who had accumulated vast experience in football administration by the time I arrived at Old Trafford. He was a wise little man, a grand little man. His advice to me about procedures was invaluable. He was an outstanding adjutant, but well aware who the commanding officer was, and that only one man could be boss.

If a manager does not make it his business to know every

19

little thing that is going on, how can he expect to complain when some little thing goes wrong? Thus there has to be a manager–chairman–board relationship, a manager–secretary relationship, a manager–player relationship, a manager–everybody relationship. He can take information from every department, and advice, and since he is the only person who has a grasp of the lot only he can make decisions. He must know what is going on all round him. The others are vital in their part, their own part.

So he must be allowed to make the decisions and it should also be acknowledged that he will not always turn out to be right. He can have private arguments with directors, trainers, players, coaches or even the tea ladies about what time he wants the tea. It is even possible to make them all feel that their arguments are quite right but for just this once 'we'll have it my way, because I have a particular reason for it which only I know about'. This will always be a valid argument *because* they all know he is the one who knows all.

Finally, for the time being at any rate, about directors. Good directors play an important part irrespective of the number of shares they hold. Good directors provide a sense of stability that runs throughout the club. Players will confirm that it is a cold coach-ride home, especially after a defeat, without at least one good director on the trip. And it is a miserable manager who has not the complete backing of the board to sustain him.

It is the manager's face that is well known to those other good judges, the spectators. They are good judges of what they see and cannot be expected to judge what they don't see.

So if anybody ever called to me on the street: 'Why don't you drop Bloggs, Matt?' how could he possibly know that perhaps some domestic upset had caused the unhappy Bloggs to play as if he had two left feet?

Because, as we shall see, players are as fallible and vulnerable as the rest of us. And it is the players and only the players, and how they play on match day, who make or break managers.

CHEEKY CHARLIE & CO.

Most footballers, like most joiners, doctors, cab-drivers and comedians have to be happy to do their jobs properly. Or at least they do a better job if they are not unhappy.

Most footballers, like most other entertainers, are emotional people. The rare morons among them, who have not the imagination to feel either very happy or very sad and are therefore less affected by emotional crises, are probably more consistent players than their more emotional fellows without ever reaching their heights or depths in performance.

Emotion has nothing to do with academics. I doubt that there is a greater proportion of moronic footballers than moronic professors. The important thing, I decided even when I was a player, is to recognize that men anywhere cannot be managed successfully without appreciating the importance of an individual to himself, to recognize that a player, however instinctively or genetically brilliant he is, or however dull he seems at taking things in, is not a machine who can simply be switched on and be expected to turn out the goods automatically.

Any footballer signed by a Football League club must have been blessed with the techniques to some degree for him to have got anywhere near the place. To make the most of them and even enhance them, the boss has to switch to his players' various wavelengths and tune in to their various problems, whether those problems are in the game or out of it.

All right, they can tell you to mind your own business if they like, if it *is* none of your business, but at least they will know you have tried.

I inherited a group of top-class talents, some of them great talents. I did not inherit a *team*, as some would have it. If eleven talents automatically equalled one team there would be no need for managers. In fact great talents need more managing. They were not mere boys. Most had been signed before the war. I suppose their average age was twenty-five. It was in October 1945 that I became Manchester United's manager. Wartime regional football was still going on. Of all the players I knew only one, and him only slightly. He was Johnny Carey, a tall, quietly-spoken yet loquacious Irishman of commanding presence. Players were still stationed here and there in the Services, and I had them for training only on Tuesday and Thursday evenings.

At once I told them we would aim for the sky, because even then I decided that if you aim only for the ceiling you might hit it and land straight on to your backside, or in other words that the short term is no use without the long term. Because I had already evolved the then revolutionary idea of growing my own footballers, as we shall see.

Meantime, the ones I had were probably as good as could be got together under one club boss anywhere – if we really did get together. So I was with them in training, probably one of the first track-suit managers, if not the first, because that is where you get to know your fellows best – at work. There you find out about those who need a touch of the whip, or soft talk, or a kick in the rump, those who just don't know when to stop work, those who need encouraging or curbing.

I also told them, remembering my own experiences of remote, office-confined managers, that my door was always open to them, and that I would do anything I could for them as long as it was within the law. They were as widely divergent in personality as any other group of people, as emotional as any other group of entertainers. I let it be known that I was concerned for them, and that if they were unhappy, for any reason, I would try to help.

Some of them said that for a start I could get them their £10 signing fee, which, quite legally, was due, but unpaid. I did that and put the sweetener on one sour point very quickly indeed.

Johnny Carey was a natural captain, who had the instinct for transmitting my wishes once the players were on the pitch, which, after all, is one of the qualities needed but not always possessed by captains. A captain does not actually need to be psychic, I suppose, but it helps if he is, and a good understanding of his manager's likes and dislikes goes a long way towards achieving the same result.

Johnny was not an outstanding inside-forward. So I switched him to wing-half, where he was much better, and then I switched him to full-back where he became one of the best of all time. I converted Johnny Aston from forward to full-back, too, and he became an England international

22

and surely, with Carey, made up the best pair of club full-backs in the business.

Carey knew the game well and was a captain by example as well as in technique. His dry sense of humour was a great help, and goodness knows you need a sense of humour, especially if you have to handle a humorist like Charlie Mitten for example.

Last-minute Charlie, we called him, because the last minute was the time this cheeky Charlie arrived, sometimes having paid a social visit to the dogs en route, greyhounds being his favourite animals at the time and for a long time after as I recall. Since he was always just in time and since greyhound racing was not illegal and he could please himself, and since he would keep the dressing room happy with his cracks, and since he was a splendid winger I could not complain about that.

Charlie Mitten could land a corner kick on a sixpence at will. He was a penalty kick taker who would ask the opposing goalkeeper which net stanchion he would like him to hit with as accurate a left foot as ever graced the game, and though, say, once in a hundred times, he might jump six feet to evade a savage lunging tackle by a full-back, he was an integral part of one of the best forward lines ever seen in these islands or any other place for that matter.

Give Charlie a rollicking and you would as often as not finish up roaring your head off with laughter. Some people you can take a bit of backchat from and it does not offend. Of such was Cheekie Charlie.

A sterner chap was Jack Rowley. I remember being told: 'You'll never handle Rowley.' Well, I can say that Jack Rowley never gave me a moment's trouble. He must rank as one of the greatest players it has been my good fortune to handle, and when I cast my mind back to some of the goals he scored I wonder how much he would be worth today. He played in four forward positions in six games for England and scored from almost every spot up to forty-five yards out from goal. His confidence on even the greatest occasions amounted almost to disdain. He was a tough player, too, and by nature perhaps inclined to be taciturn. But to me? No bother at all.

No, I don't know who could whack the ball harder, Jack Rowley or Bobby Charlton.

We had Jack Crompton in goal, a gentle and gentle-speaking chap whose soft voice belied the power of his punch, which if by accident (of course) it caught the ear of an opposing centre-forward (or one of his own full-backs), as well as the ball in the same instant, was inclined to be painful and sleep-producing if not quite lethal. He was also very good at saving penalty kicks. No goalkeeper was ever fitter than Jack, or a better clubman.

I wonder how much a club would pay for our centre-half of those days, Allenby Chilton, if he were playing today. Allen played without fuss, without frills, without noise, but with great command of his pitch. And, at about half his size, Henry Cockburn had about ten times as much to say. As a matter of fact little Henry (say about 5 ft 4 in) was as big a man as any on the pitch when the ball was in the air, and I have no doubt that even now if he worked on the Fosbury Flop he would win an Olympic Medal at the high jump.

Henry was one of the greatest competitors I ever saw, and if he thought one of his colleagues was not competing quite competitively enough it would not matter which one it was, great or not so great, big or not so big, he would give him a roasting fit for a regimental sergeant-major faced with a squad of haircuts of the Seventies. Even at team meetings, Henry's voice would be loudest, longest, and most vehement.

But despite our defensive strength it was the forward line that everybody raved about, especially after I made my first signing, Jimmy Delaney, Scottish international from Celtic, who everybody excepting me seemed to think had seen his best days. Jimmy soon disillusioned them and justified me.

Jimmy was brimful of boyish enthusiasm. He would chase the unlikely and sometimes even the impossible ball just in case. He always put himself into places that hurt the opposition, and in all was a source of great inspiration to others. He just couldn't be dull if he tried. I paid £4,000 for him and had nearly five years' excellent service out of him, and then was paid £3,100 for him by Aberdeen in 1950.

At inside-forward we had two entirely different and entirely complementary craftsmen and marksmen. For an example of the perfect goal-taker, since known as 'striker', I doubt that many have been in the same class as Stanley Pearson, a quietish, non-ebullient character, a perfect clubman. Pearson was absolutely devastating in the penalty box, but that was not all. He never gave a ball without thought behind it as well as beef, and he expected others to do the same, and if Charlie Mitten happened to be six inches out with a high centre Stan had called for, which meant that Charlie must have suffered a slight aberration, Stan would give him some stick, if not then, later. Usually, of course, if he asked for it Charlie would plonk it straight on his head. Perhaps it could be said that Charlie spoiled his colleagues in this regard. But seriously, Stan was as accurate in finishing off a move as Charlie was at providing the opportunity.

The other inside man was Johnny Morris, a wonderful ball-player who would take on opponents of all sizes and reputations, and beat them by sheer natural ability and sheer instinct. But he was not just an instinctive player, he was an excellent tactician by the very class of his moves, and as game as a pebble. Perhaps at times it seemed his ball-play was so good it got the better of his judgement. It didn't. Better to try your skill than put a hasty ball to the opposition, which, as far as the crowd is concerned, doesn't look as bad as losing it in a dribble but is quite as bad if not worse since it shows a lack of confidence which professional opposition is apt to spot.

The round, ruddy, cherubic face and big smile of this little fellow Morris was misleading, as some husky opponents misled by it found to their cost as they sprawled in a vain bid to clobber him.

Except for Delaney these were some of the characters I inherited, with all their skills, their attitudes, their emotions. We formed a quick and lasting understanding. They were all happy to call me 'boss', and, I am always touched to hear when I see any or all of them, still do.

ME v. MORRIS

It was a big disappointment to me in 1949 when Johnny Morris and I could not agree about something. I insisted on it. He would not agree. So he had to go.

Disagreement? That might be anything, it will be said. Well, what it amounted to was that Morris, youngest of the

1948 Final team, disagreed with my judgement when I did not select him for the first team in early 1949. He had not had a very happy season, what with injuries and some loss of form and he was very disgruntled indeed. He was also very disinclined to play in the reserves, leaving me in no doubt that he thought reserve team football was scarcely worth all the hard training. Of course, reserve team football is not anywhere near as demanding as League football. Only a fool would say that it is. But, carried to a logical conclusion, full-time, full-pressure training for the first team only would mean that only the first team would be fit enough and reserves would not be ready to step in. In any case a great footballer like Morris was certain to be back in the first team very quickly indeed. Probably pride was the cause of the rift, and no player worth his salt likes to be dropped.

But greater players and lesser players than Johnny Morris have been relegated to the reserves, and there will be more wherever the game is played. Anyway I insisted on being the arbiter on such subjects. He was unhappy and wanted to go.

Morris was my first signing out. There were critics of the move as, with hindsight, there have been critics of moves since. He fetched a then world-record fee of £25,000 paid by Derby County and later went to Leicester City. I have always felt he would have done even better than he did had he stayed at Manchester United.

But I had to make my point once and for all. There could be only one boss. Otherwise we should possibly have twelve bosses, and the gifted individuals I had striven to mould into a team might have disintegrated into eleven individuals again, and even eleven players who included internationals would be nothing playing as eleven individual entertainers. Much as I admire individual, spontaneous, extemporaneous brilliance, the greatest orchestras need a conductor.

As it was we remained a team. Our mutual respect was preserved. But, of course, there were times when I had to rollick one or another of them. I would do so irrespective of person. I could never be accused by lesser-known players of favouring an international. I had no favourites. I never delivered public rollickings.

But here I would like to remove an illusion, that I was too

26

soft at times with my players. My method was the appeal to an offender's conscience about the club and about me, and then a quiet but uncompromising insistence that I would not put up with any nonsense from any player in the club whatever his name was. A man can be made to squirm without bawling at him. If he cannot he is not worth keeping. I may have been on the gentle side, but, believe it or not, I have never been soft with any player. All right, patience please. I will come to George Best later.

In season 1947-8 we won the FA Cup by beating Blackpool. Many people, indeed, still call that immediate post-war side the 1948 team. It comprised: Crompton; Carey, Aston; Anderson (he vied with a Welsh international, Warner, for the right-half spot), Chilton, Cockburn; Delaney, Morris, Rowley, Pearson, Mitten.

It was a great team by any standards. Yet the First Division Championship, that true reflection of a team's greatness, eluded us for so long we thought there was a hoodoo on us. Under Don Revie, much later, Leeds United found out what it was like to miss big prizes by a whisker. I point to my first Manchester United team, who were runners-up in the First Division in 1947, 1948, 1949 and 1951, and it was 1952 before that pot came to Old Trafford.

But by then the 1948 team was no longer intact. And the future for a manager is fraught with danger, especially a manager of a championship team. Lucky the manager who does not worry. Or I should say slap-happy is the manager who doesn't worry. If he wins the First Division Championship he cannot go any higher (Europe was remote from us then) and the odds are that he will go lower. And, given five years or so, he will go straight down and out, he on his backside, the club into a division or two below. Unless he has made other arrangements. Like thinking ahead, at least five years ahead.

All teams, especially teams with players of a like age, are apt to be over the top within five years of reaching it. Buying players piecemeal is at best a chancy business, at worst a financial disaster. Buy them, yes. I have never had any doubts about that. But only to fit into a scheme that planning should have provided for.

From the start of my managership, and even before, I had envisaged my own, my very own, nursery or creche.

The pre-war method of team-building was to wait for a weakness to occur and try to repair it by buying a player or finding an outstanding one from junior football. Teenagers were a sensation if they made a First Division team. Even now Cliff Bastin is known as Boy Bastin because he got into Arsenal's team as a youth.

Now it doesn't raise a single eyebrow if half a dozen teenagers make their First Division debut in two weeks. And I like to think that I was the first to recognize and organize vital young talents as soon as they left school. Now, of course, practically every schoolboy who makes his home-town team, let alone those who make county and national schoolboy teams, is known to every Football League club scout worth his wages.

In passing, I am surprised that by now the cleverest footballers in a school cannot gain a GCE (or its equivalent) for football. I know that teachers do their best and devote much of their own spare time in helping schoolboy teams. I know that some of them are physical education specialists qualified to coach them. It seems a pity to me that a boy with the gift of natural football ability cannot get a qualification in his best subject while the mathematics expert can.

I don't say he doesn't need his maths, his geography, his English, or his music qualifications if he is multi-talented. So much the better if he is. I *do* say that football for the few who reach the top is a good profession and that if football is a boy's best subject he should be able to gain a school qualification. I recognize that a written examination's value would be quite outweighed by a practical one. But a panel of qualified coaches could be formed up and down the country to set practical examinations and to conduct them.

Some schools do not even play soccer. Who can estimate how many soccer prodigies have never even kicked a round ball? Not many, I suppose. If there are any it is talent wasted.

But that is for the future. In 1946 it was revolutionary even to *think* about getting boys straight from school. Get them early enough, I thought, and they would be trained according to some sort of pattern; in my case, the pattern I was trying constantly to create at Manchester United, in the first team and any other team, so that if a boy came through as far as his ability, courage, speed and character were concerned, he would fit into the pattern without feeling like a stranger among people painting pretty pictures he did not understand and had never seen before.

I managed to play for my country, but I wondered how many years I had wasted on the way, because if thoughtful planning and coaching and generally educating boys to play football mean anything they mean bringing him as quickly as possible, without rushing him or cutting corners, to his full potential. In other words, if a player reaches his full potential by thoughtful coaching a year before he would have reached it by the old slap-happy methods, a year has been added to his football life, and his club has saved a lot of money either in saving the fee it would cost for someone as good as he is or as an asset with a certain value.

Also a behaviour pattern is needed, and, not least, a feeling of belonging, so that a sense of proprietorship ('We murdered 'em') is engendered.

This plan I began at once. And this is where the value of delegating was to be seen. A manager has not only to be a judge of footballers. He has to be a judge of men who are judges of footballers and are themselves examples of the type of people I wanted to play for Manchester United, men of character.

But it was about a year after I took the job that my right arm arrived at Old Trafford, in the shape of a chirpy, chunky, cheery, soft-hearted, hard-boiled Welsh piano player with an Irish name and a Satchmo voice like a cement-mixer in full throttle.

JIMMY MURPHY AND ME

The battle front in Italy was only a few miles forward. We could have heard the guns in Bari, wherein I had arrived with my Army Eleven of top-class footballers like Joe Mercer, Frank Swift, Tommy Lawton, Cliff Britton, George Smith, Maurice Edelston, Willie Watson, etc., etc., had it not been for the loud entreaties of a tough little character in the act of training some other temporarily resident footballers.

I had bumped into him before. Or perhaps I should say

he had bumped into me before, when I played for Manchester City and Liverpool and he for West Bromwich Albion, since Jimmy Murphy was not averse, notwithstanding his great skill, to sitting an opponent on his bottom if by that means – and of course always within the law! – he was the more certain to relieve him of the ball. He was a master of the timing of the tackle.

But it was his attitude, his command, his enthusiasm and his whole driving, determined action and word-power that caused me to say to myself: 'He's the man for me.' He was the man I needed to help in my over-all plan for Manchester United, whom I had decided to join as manager. He was the man who would help me create a pattern that would run right through the several teams of players from fifteen years of age upwards to the first team.

I told him, if he wanted it, I had a job for him, and he was to contact me as soon as he was demobilized. About a year later he came, and an association was formed that was to last throughout my managership.

Jimmy Murphy was my first signing, as assistant-manager and chief coach. Almost at once we seemed to fit. On the face of it we may have seemed like opposites. He may have looked more excitable, more ebullient than I, though he has always shunned publicity. He may have seemed a physically tougher player and character than I, though he was as much at home with Chopin on the pianoforte as with the science of hard, uncompromising but clean tackling.

But as unlike poles attract, if unlike poles we were, we attracted. Our ideas were similar and from this understanding, my conception of a creche, a nursery, then a school with a curriculum of playing and character standards and my overall search for a pattern that would facilitate the interchanging of players from one team to another – from all these were born what eventually were known as the Busby Babes.

It could be that what either Jimmy Murphy or I lacked the other had. He would always give a straightforward opinion. He was no yes-man. But once having made a point he would accept that mine was the decision. He was forthright with never a suggestion of usurping my position. In fact he turned down many managerial jobs offered him at other clubs. If he judged a player I found that his judgements almost always confirmed mine. He was invaluable in handling boys but his value did not rest there. He could tackle the established players with the same conviction and enthusiasm.

He watched the boys and the reserves and was often my eye in watching them. In the early days when he was watching the reserves we won the Central League championship. And then he said: 'Matt, we have won the championship with our reserves but there isn't a one of them who is going to make the first team at our standard.'

In our relentless search for the best of the boys there are Busby-and-Murphy adventures in the James Bond class (without the ladies, of course). We have travelled tens of thousands of miles together. He has been my protector against pests, of whom football has its quota, my great aid in triumph and tragedy.

Among players the ones he could not stand were malingerers. He could not put up with deceivers or the chicken-hearted.

I put Bert Whalley as Jimmy's assistant. A soft-spoken, studious type, a good judge and a particularly good influence on youngsters. Bert's career had been cut short by injury. Here again, Murphy and Whalley, unlike poles, attracted. My coaching was in good hands.

Of course, I poked my nose in whenever I could. It was many years before I decided I no longer had the breath to show those young players that I could still do a bit. And there's nothing a player likes better than to have a kick at the boss. It must be the only job in which you can take a kick at the boss and not get kicked out for it. Otherwise he could accuse you of not trying hard enough.

Training stories of Jimmy Murphy, too, are legion. One I cherish concerns Jimmy in action against one of our younger players. Training has to be realistic. It is no use being gentle in practice games. That would be bad practice for the ferocious reality. This time Jimmy went across the lad with a blatant foul and the lad butted him on his backside. 'Sorry Mr Murphy,' said the lad, and Jimmy said, 'Come here. Don't let me hear you say "Sorry" again. I fouled you. You were quite right.'

If the manager or coach cannot take a bump at practice he shouldn't be in the practice game. He would be better teaching pantomime fairies. One facet of football coaching is how to cope with the clogger, legitimately, that is. Of course.

We had Tom Curry and Bill Inglis as trainers, priceless with their experience and their genius for keeping the dressing room happy. Tom Curry was so fond of Old Trafford that he used to bring his open razor to the ground so that he would not waste time shaving at home. If the team played badly he would leave his open razor on the dressing room table and say: 'Help yourself, lads.'

Sounds macabre, but Tom was one of the gentlest men in football, one of the finest Christians I ever met. He was a Church of England man. But whenever we were playing away from home and were away on the Sunday he would go round to every player, of whatever persuasion, and say: 'Now don't forget to get along to the service.'

Here I might dispel an illusion which continued to get back to me over many years of my managership. Often I have heard that a man has said of some player: 'Oh, he'll be all right. He's a Roman Catholic.' This, of course, because I am a Roman Catholic. But it is a most unchristian thing to say for a start. And I should not have to reply to it, as I do now, that never has a man's religion influenced anybody's decisions at Manchester United in any way. I have always believed that a person's religion is in his mind and in his heart.

ROGER BYRNE

When the super-scout, Louis Rocca, died, I gave the job to a great little ferret, Joe Armstrong, who, when I was at Manchester City as a player, was doing a bit of scouting there. He too fitted into the scheme of things. The fact that Joe was a gentleman ferret was a great help in dealing with parents. He or one of his team would spot a lad. Jimmy and/or I would check him out.

Sometimes we got news from surprising sources. Joe Mercer, the Everton, Arsenal and England wing-half and later Sheffield United, Aston Villa, Manchester City and Coventry City manager, was still playing when he was asked to coach the England schoolboy team. When we were chatting one day Joe said that among the many promising boys one was outstanding. This was a boy called Duncan Edwards. Joe had heard Duncan say in the dressing room that he wanted to go to Manchester United. So when people ask me how we came to sign Duncan Edwards, one of the greatest all-round players in history, when the boy came from Dudley, in Worcestershire, the answer is, he wanted to come.

How did we get Bobby Charlton? He wanted to come to Manchester United.

I believe they wanted to come to Manchester United because we had won a reputation for being the best club for the best boy players. Not all were set on joining Manchester United before all others. Then Joe Armstrong, Jimmy Murphy, or I would try talking them into believing how good we were as a club for the best boys.

We didn't sign all the best ones, but we managed more than our share, so that in our midst, ever maturing, ever growing into the Old Trafford pattern of play and behaviour, we had an extraordinary number of youths. In their maturing they took in winning the FA Youth Cup in 1953, '54, '55, '56 and '57.

In the meantime we had brought along a boy who matured into a wonderful successor, as the captain, to Johnny Carey. Around about the time I was trying to persuade Brian Statham to play football for Manchester United, which request he turned down on the grounds that he wanted to concentrate on cricket, thus showing excellent judgement, we signed Roger Byrne, a young local outside-left. As we had converted Johnny Carey and Johnny Aston from forwards to international full-backs, so we did with Roger Byrne. Simple proof of Byrne's quite outstanding skill is that I never saw either the great Stan Matthews or the great Tom Finney do anything against him. Greater tribute can no full-back have than this. There was never a faster full-back than Byrne.

But his graduation to becoming a great captain did not happen overnight. He was a strong and strong-willed young man, and, as many young men are, he was a bit headstrong to begin with.

Manchester United were playing Atlas, the Mexican

champions, in Los Angeles, and Atlas were a rough, tough lot. Seeing how things were going I told Johnny Carey to instruct the team to keep their heads, keep together and keep calm. This he did, but Roger defied him and was sent off.

I was annoyed about this. I did not like Manchester United players to be sent off, though I know before anybody jumps that we have had our share of these unhappy occurrences. I especially did not like my players to be sent off abroad, where club and national reputations suffer more than the individual players' reputations. Nor did I like my instruction or my captain's instructions to be forgotten, even allowing for provocation, of which there was plenty.

So I had to make my point once more. I was the boss. We would do it my way. I told Roger that he must apologize to Johnny Carey or I would send him home the next day. I would give him two hours to do it in. No more than fifteen minutes later Johnny Carey came to me and said: 'Roger has been to apologize.'

So Roger rose in my estimation, high in it though he already was. I knew it was only a lapse into a headstrong state that had caused his dismissal. Now he had shown that he was big enough to apologize. I believe the whole incident was a part of Roger Byrne's growing-up into becoming another of the game's great captains.

The very young footballer will get into mischief as the very young office boy or apprentice will. The trouble with footballers is that the club is hurt more than the individual.

Even that model for all footballers everywhere they play the game, Bobby Charlton, when he was a mere lad, I once had to put right. I had heard he had been seen to have a drink of beer. As I say, he was very young. So I sent for him and I told him: 'If I ever hear you have been drinking beer again before you are old enough you will be for it.'

It was a long time before he had his next glass of beer, and certainly not before he was old enough. He likes a glass now, I think. But who doesn't? In fact the sweating these fellows do in training now makes the odd glass of beer quite harmless.

I remember once that several members of my first team stayed out of our hotel a little longer than I had laid down. I could trust my players not to overdo anything. But I had the club name and my own authority to think about. So I gave them a brisk but quiet speech in the lounge. 'If any one of you ever stays out longer than I say again, and I don't care what your name is or your reputation as a player, I will get rid of you.'

I am told one player said after it all: 'The boss made us squirm.' In fact as I told players from time to time over the years: 'I have no spying system, but you can be sure that if you do anything wrong somebody will tell me.' And it is true.

The ideal, I suppose, would be for footballers to live like Trappist monks. But if they were so gifted they would all *be* Trappist monks. Footballers are ordinary mortals with ordinary mortals' weaknesses and are as varied in their intellects as they are varied in skills. Yet, induced, of course, by simple commonsense, footballers, *per capita*, have a greater sense of dedication, a more general willingness to knuckle down to discipline, I feel sure, than most sections of the population.

Even the most enthusiastic devotee among them, the footballer who is normally so fond of training that he gives an impression he cannot be given too much of it, must occasionally be bored to the back teeth with the constant repetitious, physical effort, however varied the modern top-class coach and trainer try to make the work. I do not have to be reminded that amateur athletes train daily, voluntarily, and without reward, up to a hundred miles a week. But this, I feel, is a self-challenge, a determination, at least to begin with, to beat their previous best, in other words beating themselves being the first course in trying to beat the opposition. Or even the second, third or sixteenth course. I may be wrong but I believe many athletes find no difficulty in living with themselves, living with their own thoughts, and that, in a word, many of them are 'loners'.

Footballers, like runners, have to beat the pain barrier to get anything from their training or any success in actual performance. But footballers, unlike athletes, are more likely to flourish or even survive in the pack. Few footballers are loners, and it is as well, since colleagues are as necessary to their training as they are in a match. Their performance itself is influenced by the same ego urge of the athlete who wants to win a prize, or the woodcarver who

35

exhibits his carvings. They all like to show off a bit, to display their talents.

Some weeks for a footballer are more pressurized than others. But at the end of any week of training the time before a match, during the last few moments, or the whole morning for some, even the sleepless night before for others, most players are pinched with tension, as actors have their own collywobbles on a first night (or even a 551st night).

They have a longing to relax from it all, to do something to take the mind away from it. It is part of a manager's job to try to find ways of doing this – films, golf, cards in the coach and so on. One wrong way of reducing tension is to go boozing in a night-club. Another is simply to stay out longer than orders permit. These methods may well take off tension, but they take the 'edge' off performance, too. Such novelties must be stamped upon no matter whose toes are bruised. But whatever the transgression, serious, not-so-serious, or merely frivolous, I do not subscribe to to the idea of public flogging.

Private flagellation is as painful and as lastingly effective as the public variety. But it preserves the offender's public dignity as well as the flagellant's and the club's. Players' extra-curricular activities are sometimes made public whether the manager likes it or not, usually because the Press have got wind of them. And, since footballers are public figures who get much and good publicity from the Press, the Press cannot really be blamed for that.

But public punishment, I am inclined to believe, is sometimes a sop to the pride of the man who decides to inflict it. In other words, 'I'm the boss, I'll show 'em, and I'll let it be seen I've shown 'em.' Hence the illusion that I was a bit soft with my players.

Footballers' transgressions are rare. That is why such a meal is made of them when they do come out in the open. All right, all right, I *will* put George in his place, his right place in this book, that is!

The fact is that my senior players posed few behaviour problems, not only because I always told them that whatever they might do that I would not approve of they could be sure somebody would tell me about it. My players kept on the straight-and-narrow by habit because we brought them up that way.

Bringing up the young boys is the thing that really matters. It would have been ungrateful, no, it would have been immoral, for me to talk parents into allowing their boys to come along to Manchester to live and to play football if I had not immediately assumed responsibility for their well-being.

So I became their foster father, a huge responsibility, and one that was never far from my mind. I had to *care* how they were going on. They had to *see* I cared how they were going on. Fifteen is a formative age for boys. If they were to acquire anything from Old Trafford I was determined it would not be bitterness.

The *training* of boys is not all. At least there is far more to it than mere physical and technical football training. They have to be housed with and cared for by people who will take them into their family as if they were their own. Manchester United were once fined for paying £1 10s. over the specified fee for such care. I trust St Peter will not hold it against us!

Great care has to be taken that the boys do not spend all their money, and that they make good use of their spare time, and to do this we found them jobs, or put them on courses, or set them to trades that would help if by seventeen years of age, and notwithstanding their embryonic talents, they had not developed to Football League standards and were not signed as full-time professionals.

There is not as much spare time for footballers now as there used to be. Playing billiards is not the best way to use it. Not many people make a living out of playing billiards.

Boys are the very lifeblood of the Football League. They are the very *life* of their parents. The parents must not be let down. They are the ones who feel every heartbeat of their fledglings when they have left the nest at a mere fifteen years of age. And the real heartbreak comes when, after every test has failed, or even if half the tests have failed, or even a quarter of the tests have failed, it is decided – and in Manchester United's case it was if I had decided acting on my own judgement and the advice of my aides – that the boy is not going to reach the standard. Then the parents have to be told. And the boy has to be told. I do not know which of the three finds it hardest to bear, the boy, his parents, or the manager, who has formed his own affection for the lad and whose judgement has proved to be wrong.

But I do not know any greater joy in football than to see first the seed show through, then the lissom shoot growing, then the healthy young plant, and finally the full bloom and hear the acclaim that attends it. Then and only then can the football foster father join in with the parents and say: 'That's my boy.'

THE BABES

Came the time that my first team began to go over the top, over the peak in their playing careers; not all at once but the signs were there. We played a friendly at Kilmarnock and I drafted seven of my youngsters into the team. We won 3-0.

My old team had won the championship the last season (1951-2). It looked a bit chancy to chop it to bits. But at Huddersfield the following Saturday I kept to the youngsters and we drew 2-2. And I stuck it out. The future was more important than the present that season. We finished eighth. Next season we were fourth, then fifth, which was not perfect, but a remarkable affirmation that my pattern system was right. The pieces dropped out, the pieces dropped in.

We won the championship in 1956 and again in 1957, by which time we had augmented our natural resources. I had never expected to be lucky enough or clever enough to find eleven great players for one team at one time. Thus I had bought a goalkeeper, Ray Wood, for £6,000 from Darlington in 1950, Johnny Berry for £25,000 from Birmingham in 1951, and Tommy Taylor for £29,999 from Barnsley in 1953, an insignificant outlay compared with the priceless value of a collection of home-bred kids the quality of which had never before, I believe, been assembled in one club anywhere in the world.

The Busby-Murphy cloak-and-dagger (or perhaps it should be cloak-and-patter) stuff could not be better exemplified than in our quest to sign Tommy Taylor.

I had sent Jimmy to see him play. He reported. So I went

to see him play for Barnsley against Birmingham. After half an hour I had seen enough. He was the boy to complete my pattern.

Other clubs were interested. So Jimmy and I stayed in a pub in the Barnsley area for two days and nights, trying to keep hidden. For a breath of fresh air we would slip in my car out into the countryside.

One afternoon we decided to pass a couple of hours in the cinema. We knew one manager at least was in the district trying to sign Tommy. So Jimmy tipped the girl who collected our tickets and asked her to let us know if a tall fellow wearing a trilby and a fawn overcoat came in. Sure enough a few minutes later along she came and pointed. It was our friend all right. We sat back and enjoyed the film.

Anyway the time came when I rang Mr Joe Richards, later Sir Joe, the president of the Football League and chairman of Barnsley, who wanted £30,000 for Tommy. But I told Joe I didn't want the lad, for his own sake, tagged a £30,000 player (a large sum in the 1950s). So we agreed to a fee of £29,999. I could then in all truth, in answer to questions, say the fee was less than £30,000.

In fact we were there so long and we had so many cups of tea that I gave the tea lady a £1 tip, so Tommy Taylor did cost us £30,000 (if I remembered to put that quid on my expenses, which I am sure I did. I'll have to check!).

The full-backs, Billy Foulkes and Roger Byrne, were England players, Eddie Colman, a local lad, was making even old heads chuckle with his confident wiggle-hips wing-half play, Jackie Blanchflower was an Irish international, Mark Jones was a splendid centre-half, Duncan Edwards, England 'man' as an eighteen-year-old boy, Liam Whelan, superb ball-playing Republic of Ireland international, Dennis Viollet, later an England international, David Pegg, England international, Bobby Charlton, just getting into the team and to become a World Cup winner, Geoff Bent, another brilliant prospect, and even younger ones like Nobby Stiles, Johnny Giles, Nobby Lawton, Alex Dawson, Mark Pearson, and so on, coming along, getting into the pattern.

We won the League in seasons 1955-6 (by eleven points) and 1956-7 as I said, and lost the 1957 FA Cup in the

Final through an injury to Ray Wood. But we had also become the first England team to go into the European Cup. Chelsea, champions in 1954-5, had turned down the chance to enter, accepting the Football League's advice. I accepted Europe when we won the English title in 1956 and we reached the European Cup semi-final in 1957 to be beaten by the then great Real Madrid. And we reached the semi-final again in 1958.

Then suddenly, cruelly, eight of those wonderful, precocious Busby Babes were torn from our grasp and England wept. No, the world wept.

MUNICH

Eight Manchester United players, three of the club's staff, and eight of nine newspaper representatives, were among the dead after an aircraft crashed on take-off at Munich on February 6, 1958, during the return trip from a European Cup-tie in Belgrade. The players were: Roger Byrne, Geoffrey Bent, Eddie Colman, Duncan Edwards, Mark Jones, David Pegg, Tommy Taylor and Liam Whelan. The staff members were: Walter Crickmer (Secretary), Tom Curry (Trainer) and Bert Whalley (Coach). The newspaper representatives were: Alf Clarke, Don Davies, George Follows, Tom Jackson, Archie Ledbrooke, Henry Rose, Eric Thompson and Frank Swift.

The world still wept for Manchester United, decimated at Munich. My life had been spared, though it still hung on only by a thread. I wanted to die. It was not only the physical agony. I had critical chest and leg injuries. Anaesthetics were out because of the damage to my chest. So only unconsciousness relieved the pain of the appalling injuries to my right leg and foot. But in my consciousness I wanted to die because my tortured mind kept saying: 'Was I to blame?'

Memories kept jumping in at me. Chelsea had heeded the Football League's advice and had not entered the European Cup. I had not heeded the League's advice when we had the chance of going into Europe and I had taken Manchester United into the European Cup.

The inner voice kept on saying: 'If I had not taken them into Europe those eight Busby Babes and the other victims would be with us still.'

And this was not all. The voice admonished: 'I should not have allowed the pilot to make that third attempt at take-off.'

But with the diminishing of the physical agony my more rational mind put up an unanswerable defence against both my inner voice's charges. My rational mind said: 'A football life is a travelling life. Tragedy could have struck us in a train, in a coach, or even walking across a road. And, after all, effects on human beings are from a million small causes dating from the year dot.

'And who am I, who was I, to presume to tell an expert pilot how to do his job?' I knew less about aeroplanes than he knew about football. That was certain.

I have tried to collect my thoughts, my recollections of the whole nightmare from those moments waiting in Munich Airport. Here they are:

People who fly many journeys know the sounds. The drone of the Elizabethan's engines exploded into a roar and the big aircraft charged along the runway. Nothing unusual about this. Some people, whose courage in face of any other calls upon it would never fail them, will not fly in aeroplanes at all.

Those who *do* fly in them, often, will know that this first moment, when the engine's drone becomes a crack of thunder announcing take-off time, gives a little twist to the most hardened stomach, a twist of tension, a feeling of, 'This is it, God help us.' Men will hide their fears, since no man likes to look 'chicken', but those fears are there all right, until, paradoxically, the aircraft is up in the 'safety' of the air.

But we did not take off. The roar returned to a drone, we turned round, and idled back along the runway.

If take-off brings on that twinge of tension, take-off failure does nothing to reduce it. But the time came when we roared along that runway again. And again the roar stopped, and we droned and turned again and idled back. Two take-off failures were alarming.

41

Had we been in a depressed state after defeat we might have been more apprehensive. As it was we had just won our way into the semi-final of the European Cup, a most cheerful situation.

We settled back yet again, and again we sped in a great din of engines. But we sped on and on and on and my thoughts sounded just like that – 'On and on and on and on' – until they changed to 'Too long, too long, too long, too long!' We were not going up.

My next glimpse in the mists of memory is of throwing out my arms in a pathetic attempt at self-protection, and then of the world crashing in on us.

Next I see through those mists a brief, a fleeting glance in a snatch of consciousness. I see a big room with several covered bodies in it. I think I can hear now a doctor looking down at one of them and saying: 'This one is dead.' I have always had a feeling it was Frank Swift, I don't know why. Then I heard Professor Maurer telling the doctor to keep quiet.

Jimmy McGuire, President of the United States Football Association, arrived in Munich next morning. I was very ill but not too ill to recognize my dear old friend. He spoke to me. I nodded. It was enough.

I know now that little hope was held for me. The Professor banished everybody from my bedside. He did not want anything to knock me back. All I could feel, all I knew about at that time, was the pain. Then day after day, instinctively, gradually I began to feel that something terrible had happened. But it was not until about two weeks after the crash that I overheard a clergyman saying: 'Duncan Edwards is dead.' And then, for the first time, it really dawned on me. I really knew, though I had no idea what, that something even more terrible than I could imagine had struck, and that they were keeping it from me.

My wife, Jean, was at my bedside. When I asked what had happened she changed the subject. 'Don't worry,' she would say. 'Don't talk. I'm supposed to do the talking.'

Finally I could stand it no longer. I said: 'Jean I want to know. I want to know the worst. For my peace of mind.' So began a new torture, for Jean and for me. I would name a name and without saying a word she would nod or shake her head. When even now I think about her feelings at that

42

time, let alone mine, in those dreadful moments of telling me about those poor kids, and those other lost friends, I could weep, and I am not by nature a weeping man.

This new torture, this constant mental torture, knocked me back and I was as near the brink as ever.

I was spared, but even if I survived how could I face the loved ones of the lads who were not spared? 'Was I to blame? Was I to blame? Why can't I die?'

The physical agony remained without let-up. Coughing was painful even to think about. When coughing, as I inevitably did, the pain was so excruciating that an old ward sister used to lean over me and I pulled most fearful faces and when it was over she would say: 'Wunderbar, Mr Boosby.'

Lung punctures, broken-bone manipulation, torn-flesh repairs without anaesthetics were a regular drill of undiminishing horror.

But even when I had talked myself out of my self-condemnation and self-blame on those two counts, my mental state was worse than the physical pain. 'I will never go back into football,' I would say, and this went on for weeks. But Jean, in her wisdom again, said: 'I don't think you are being fair to the people who have lost their loved ones. And I am sure those who have gone, too, would have wanted you to carry on.'

This plea went straight to the crux of the real matter. Jean's wisdom, commonsense and logic won. And had I not some more foster sons to look after? I must not let them down. Or their parents.

From that moment I wanted to live.

FROM THE ASHES

Professor George Maurer, chief surgeon at the Rechts der Isar Hospital, Munich, who had done much to keep me alive, said it would be of great benefit to me if I convalesced for a few weeks in the Black Forest or at Interlaken. I owed it to him at least not to knock myself back yet again by doing anything silly, like going home too soon and trying to rush the process of my rehabilitation.

I chose Interlaken, and there, with Jean at my side, and breathing the good, clean, fresh air, I gradually felt better. Hobbling along on my stick I was by no means right physically, but my mental improvement was constant if slow.

Came the time I made up my mind to go home and prepare myself for the start of the 1958–9 season, the job of building United yet again, this time from the ashes.

But resting in Interlaken was one thing and facing Old Trafford another. When I approached the ground and moved over the bridge along which our supporters had squeezed, fifty abreast in their tens of thousands to shout for us I could scarcely bear to look. I knew the ghosts of the Babes would still be there, and there they are still, and they will always be there as long as those who saw them still cross the bridge, young, gay, red ghosts on the green grass of Old Trafford.

We had lost the bulk of a team whose potential knew no bounds. The 'Babes' team who won the First Division championship in 1955–6 season by an astonishing margin of eleven points had an average age of about twenty-one. They were scarcely weaned in the big game. The marks of the nursery cradle were still on them but they did not show. Only Johnny Berry, Tommy Taylor and Ray Wood had been signed from other clubs.

Possibly their peak performance was in beating Anderlecht 10–0 in our first European Cup home tie, but that was a kid's peak compared with what was surely to come with maturity. One almost immediate huge peak I believed was denied them by the disaster, which occurred when we were returning from drawing with Red Star of Belgrade and so clinching our place in the European Cup semi-final. Young as the Babes still were they were quite capable of winning the trophy. We were second in the League and in the fifth round of the FA Cup and it was well within the power of these prodigies to have won the lot. But not only that. I am convinced that I could have sat back and watched this collection of infants pile up a list of championships and cups for years to come. They were surely the greatest group of young footballers in one team ever gathered together.

In Walter Crickmer, Tom Curry and Bert Whalley we had lost backroom men of inestimable value and experience. Jimmy Murphy was not with the Munich party. He was doing his job with the Welsh international team. That is why poor Bert Whalley was there.

And the newspaper world, at least the Northern part of it, had lost the cream of its football writers. Alf Clarke (*Manchester Evening Chronicle*), Donnie Davies (*Manchester Guardian*), George Follows (*Daily Herald*), Tom Jackson (*Manchester Evening News*), Archie Ledbrooke (*Daily Mirror*), Henry Rose (*Daily Express*) and Eric Thompson (*Daily Mail*) were not only top-quality newspapermen with vast experience. They were men of quality as people. It is a remarkable truth that in a profession whose very nature demands that friendships with the subjects of their stories must occasionally be stretched to the limits I never heard before their death or since a single word that cast doubt upon their integrity.

They were as different as footballers are different. Henry Rose combined a sense of theatre with brilliance as a reporter, Eric Thompson was as talented with his sketchbook as his notebook, Don Davies was an essayist in the Carlus class, George Follows, younger than the rest, composed fine prose and was at the mere threshold of a great career.

Archie Ledbrooke was a wise and highly-respected observer, Alf Clarke and Tom Jackson, as the local evening papers' men and therefore even closer to United than the others, loved the club with a passion born of virtually living with the United players, and (although they would have indignantly denied they were anything but impartial) were said to limp if any of our players was kicked.

Different styles, different operators yes, but exactly the same in that they were straight shooters to a man. They left a tremendous gap for young men to fill.

And there was Frank Swift, former Manchester City and England goalkeeper – some would say the best ever England goalkeeper and I would not argue with them – one of the greatest, warmest, jolliest footballer-personalities who ever laced a boot. He died at Munich in his role as representative of the *News of the World*.

The lone Press survivor was Frank Taylor (*News Chronicle*), whose severe injuries did not stop him from trying to cheer us from his hospital bed and who happily is still going strong.

45

Meanwhile at Old Trafford Jimmy Murphy had done a great job with a patchwork collection, without semblance of the pattern we had sought and achieved twice in little over a decade. What pattern *could* be achieved with so many integral parts wrenched from the whole? But the patchwork collection beat Sheffield Wednesday, West Bromwich Albion and Fulham to get to the FA Cup Final against Bolton Wanderers at Wembley, where we lost by two goals scored by Nat Lofthouse, one of which, controversial to say the least, he achieved by knocking our goalkeeper, Harry Gregg, over the line. Nat scored some great goals in his time. That was not one of them.

The United team was: Gregg; Foulkes, Greaves; Goodwin, Cope, Crowther; Dawson, Taylor (E.), Charlton, Viollet, Webster.

Harry Gregg, whom I signed from Doncaster Rovers in late 1957, Bobby Charlton, Dennis Viollet, Bill Foulkes, Albert Scanlon and Ken Morgans had survived the crash, and Jimmy Murphy made emergency signings in Stan Crowther, who had played well against us in the previous year's Cup Final, and little Ernie Taylor, a wonderful ball-player and general but, alas, nearing the end of his career.

We had more babes in the creche, not yet ready for the big, hard world of the First Division. We never believed in rushing them in. But some of them had to be rushed.

I bought Albert Quixall from Sheffield Wednesday for £45,000, but the business of team picking was largely experimenting with what we had left. Yet astonishingly we finished runners-up in the 1958-9 season and gave Stan Cullis's Wolverhampton champions a fright or two in doing so. But I did not delude myself that we were there among the great teams again. I knew it was going to take us the best part of five years to re-create the old pattern if ever we could.

One thing I was determined to do. It was to keep the name of Manchester United on people's lips. We had always to look as if we were *doing* something. Having been the greatest we would not settle for anything less, and our supporters who had roared us on to Wembley immediately after the crash deserved nothing less. The matter of feeling important is as important to a supporter as to a player. Supporters claim proprietorship of a team – 'We played a blinder' or 'We had a stinker' – and why not? It is their money we are spending. If we are a club and a club is people the supporters are our sponsors. They pay for the privilege of claiming success if the team wins and for playing hell if it loses. All I would ever ask for is their patience when there seems to be inaction and action is needed, and their understanding that it is not always possible from the outside to see what is really a good reason from the inside.

FILLING THE GAP

At that time the glamour club of the whole football world was Real Madrid. I have said my rule was to reach for the sky, so I wanted Real Madrid at Old Trafford. I wanted them as an experience for my team. I wanted them to keep Manchester United in the public eye. I wanted them to give our supporters that important feeling. I could give them nothing better than United *v*. The Kings of the Football World.

So I took a trip to Real Madrid's headquarters. We had already an affinity with them formed during our European Cup adventures, and with the man who had made this mighty club, Mr Santiago Bernabeu. We met, with Real's business manager, and I asked them to bring their team to Old Trafford for a friendly.

Real Madrid at that time were commanding about £12,000 to visit any club for a match, an enormous sum then. I said the crash had ruined us financially as well as physically and I would be grateful if they would take this into consideration. Mr Bernabeu turned to the business manager and said: 'We must treat Matt and Manchester United generously.' They did, and Real Madrid came at less than half price.

And they walloped us 6–1.

In doing so, they confirmed what I knew – that we had a long, long way to go to close the gap, the gap between us and the sky.

Our achievement in finishing second in that first season after the crash was in football terms a miracle. I would not take a thing from the brave efforts of our players. I acknowl-

47

edged that our supporters, in a wave of emotion that surely has never been experienced in football before, almost willed us to win when winning seemed impossible. But I knew that until the real shape, according to the real pattern, had been re-created we were, in terms of Manchester United, nothing. I knew our position was false.

Some of the new Babes were coming along quite nicely, but in the season 1959–60 I decided that they were a little short in the strength department. I needed a dominant, energetic man in what came to be known later as the back four. Around this time I heard mention that Maurice Setters might be leaving West Bromwich Albion.

Just the lad for me, I thought. I admired him as a fighter (in the nicest sense of the word, of course), as a player who hated losing (I am afraid good losers gather no medals except in boys' magazines), a player who could not stand idlers.

One day when I had taken the team to Blackpool for a break I asked Bobby Charlton what he thought about Maurice Setters, with whom he had played Under-23 international games. 'I'm sure Maurice would do us a lot of good,' said Bobby, so I signed him in January 1950 for £30,000 and he did exactly that, in fact a splendid job.

Maurice was a fiery sort of character besides being a fiery sort of player, and there were a few occasions when I had to straighten him up (or calm him down, take your choice). But he would always take it from me. And whatever was said we did not lose one iota of respect for each other. He was a man's man. He knew he needed the calming down treatment at times.

He served us well. A good sergeant-major type. And we finished seventh. Quite respectable.

Next season (1960-1) I was still searching around, particularly for a full-back, having lost the great Roger Byrne and his deputy, Geoff Bent, in the crash, and having moved Bill Foulkes to centre-half. We were a bit thin in the full-back department.

I wanted an experienced man who would cool things down a bit at the back. The one I had in mind was Noel Cantwell, a West Ham favourite. I paid £29,500 for him. He was experienced. He had a magnificent, athlete's physique. He was a classical full-back rather than a des-troyer. He always insisted on using the ball, creating, and spurned belting it up the pitch to nobody in particular. He always took a sensible view of situations, so that players respected him and cooled down as near as they could to his temperature.

When he became captain he was a straight-talking in-termediary between the players and me without being a militant one. His personality indeed was perfectly reflected in his play. If he made a suggestion it could be guaranteed to be worth thinking about.

He was captain of Eire, too, of course, and played almost everywhere for them – full-back, centre-half, even centre-forward. He was indeed the nearest approach to Johnny Carey that Eire or Manchester United ever had. Greater tribute I cannot pay than that.

In that season another young Irishman, Tony Dunne, played three League games, yet another, Johnny Giles, added twenty-three to the ten games he had the pre-vious season, a Manchester tiddler called Nobby Stiles played twenty-six League games and again we finished seventh.

In 1961-2 we dropped to fifteenth, but we reached the FA Cup semi-final, losing 3-1 to Tottenham Hotspur, who had won the Cup and League double the year before and who went on to win the FA Cup again and finish third in the League in 1961-2. Spurs were then regarded as nothing less than majestic.

Despite our poor League position I could see that things were beginning to take shape. But, pondering in between the million and one jobs a manager has to do if he insists on knowing absolutely every little thing that goes on, which I still did, though I was not by any means one hundred per cent fit, I decided that one player at least I needed, and that was a striking forward around the eighteen-yard box to line up with David Herd, a hard-shooting Scottish inter-national I had signed from Arsenal for £40,000 in July 1961. David had inherited his mighty shot from his father, Alex, with whom I played for Manchester City. Whose shot was the mightier, David's or his dad's, we shall never know.

After that Spurs' match and my cogitations that followed it, I knew the man I wanted. He didn't play in England. He didn't play in Britain. He played for Torino, whom he had joined from Manchester City. The great Denis Law no less. But what a song and dance there was and what mileage I covered in trying to get him!

THE ITALIAN JOB

I had long admired Denis Law. It was I who brought him at only seventeen into the Scotland international team, which I managed for a brief spell, a job I had to give up for health reasons and because of my many commitments with Manchester United. So I knew him well and I knew his football well.

In fact I tried to sign him when he was in Huddersfield Town's youth team. I said to Andy Beattie, then manager at Leeds Road: 'I'd like to give you £10,000 for that young fellow Law.' The offer was declined with thanks.

Anyway, while Denis was playing for Torino he was chosen to represent the Italian League against the Football League at Old Trafford. (Incidentally, the Football League is what is called the English League in Scotland, Ireland and Wales, so if ever I slip into the Scottish habit of calling it the English League may I be forgiven. In fact, I have even been known to call the FA Cup the English Cup. Tut, tut!)

At the banquet after the match I ran into Denis Law and said to him: 'How do you like playing in Italy, Denis?'

'I don't like it. Why don't you come and buy me?' he said.

Mine was a perfectly simple question which any man would ask any man. I didn't realize how desperately Denis wanted to come back home.

Later I met Emil Ostereicher, the manager of the Italian League team, in George Sturrup's home in Hampstead, George being a great friend of Manchester United's. We discussed Denis. Of course Emil knew of Law's unhappy state of mind, but he began talking in astronomical figures like £200,000, which was an almost unbelievable fee ten years ago. We decided to leave it to Emil to discuss the matter with Torino officials.

Next step (step, I say!) was a trip to Amsterdam to meet Torino's president, Angela Filippone, the night before

Benfica of Portugal beat Real Madrid 5-3 in the European Cup Final. He talked in enormous figures, too. But we had one advantage. Denis *hated* playing in Italy. It was now an obsession with him. The meeting was again postponed. They would contact us.

An arrangement was made to meet Mr Filippone, this time in Lausanne. At least we *expected* Mr Filippone, but he didn't arrive, and I was fuming that I had brought an old man like our chairman Harold Hardman so far on a wasted journey, not to mention having wasted time I could ill afford to waste anyway from my seven-days-a-week, sixteen-hours-a-day job.

Luckily for me I later ran into a great friend in Italy, Gigi Peronace, the 'Italian spy' as the English Press dubbed him for his exploits in taking Denis Law, Joe Baker, John Charles and others to Italy. To my vast disappointment Gigi said: 'You will not sign Law.' I said we were *there* to sign him, but he said there was trouble at Torino about the possibility of Denis being sold. He was right. We were back where we started. But I said to Gigi: 'See what you can do. Find out the position and let us know.'

Eventually we went to Majorca for a tournament and I had a message that the Torino people would contact me there. In Majorca then the phone services were anything but perfect. I waited for two days in the foyer of an hotel for a call that never came. Well, it seemed like never, but surprise, surprise, at last one morning a call came from Mr Filippone's office asking would we go to Turin, Harold Hardman and I and a director, Louis Edwards, who would join us from England.

We took a plane to Geneva. A car would pick us up there, the three of us. The Italian Press had got hold of it, and a few English 'stringers' out there. A crowd of them waited for us, and to lose them we ran into a garage. We succeeded in putting them off the scent.

Over the mountains in the car we sped. It was getting more and more like a movie every minute. We arrived in Turin at 11 p.m. With a movie plot like this, could Mr Filippone be there at last? He couldn't, and he wasn't. But his second-in-command was, which gentleman was adamant that Denis was about to sign for Juventus for £200,000. Our idea was about £80,000 maximum.

51

After a quiet but no less vehement bit of top-blowing by me and another blast for making me drag old Harold Hardman through a long, perilous journey for nothing, we were sunk again. Midnight, after such a dash, is not the best time to get shocks like that.

The measure of Denis Law's dislike of the Italian scene I can now illustrate. Denis could have added about £20,000 to his bank balance by signing for Juventus. But I learned that when he was taken to see the Juventus people he said he was not signing for them and that he was emphatically going home to Aberdeen. And he went!

All this and, for us, nothing to show for it.

The epic resumed in July 1962 when Gigi Peronace called me to say that he had been appointed by Torino to come to England and negotiate with us. And we signed Denis Law for a then record fee of £115,000. In doing so we made sure that Manchester City were paid from it the part of the fee Torino still owed them for his transfer.

At £115,000 Denis Law proved one of my best and cheapest signings. Late that same 1962-3 season I signed Pat Crerand from Celtic for £43,000, and so acquired for Manchester United another topclass player and selfless clubman.

And we won the FA Cup.

But we also narrowly escaped the embarrassing drop into the Second Division, finishing only fourth from the bottom, three points above Manchester City, who went down.

Fourth from bottom was a long, long way from the sky. Nearer the cellar in fact. But the Cup Final showed that the pieces were forming some pattern at last.

In the League we had an incredibly frustrating time. We knew we were in the process of knitting together, that the pattern was there and almost all the pieces fitting snugly. But we simply could not get a result. It seemed incredible to us that with a team of our class we were near the bottom of the table. All this was typified in a League game against Leicester City.

Denis Law scored a hat-trick, including one of those inimitable goals with an overhead kick that went in before anybody could see what was going on. And we lost 4-3. It didn't surprise me when Denis said to me after the match: 'What have we got to do to win?' And I said: 'As long as

we keep playing football the results are bound to come.'
When I said 'playing football' it may seem as if I was saying
nothing at all. But my players knew what I meant. They
knew I meant playing football the Manchester United way,
which was constructive football, attacking football, team
football but with scope for spontaneous moves of surprise
by the individuals capable of making something out of
nothing – surprise, that is, to the onlooker but not to the
class players around them. But football can floor the
greatest. A blade of grass can make the difference between a
goal and a near miss, and those blades of grass sometimes
do that very thing with depressing monotony. We couldn't
do right with our blades of grass, the opposition couldn't do
wrong.

Excuses are always being made about football. 'The ball
didn't run for us,' etc., etc., etc. And nobody realizes more
than I that a team must lift itself off the floor and make its
own luck. There is no point at all in making excuses if the
players you have are not good enough.

But I knew our players were good enough, if not yet with
the complete pattern I aimed at, and I knew they had been
playing well enough to have won many games they lost.

The public did not seem to agree, and Leicester were well
fancied to beat us at Wembley. Leicester presumably fancied themselves too. It was reported that they even rehearsed
receiving the Cup! But football should have taught everybody concerned in it – though I am afraid it hadn't then,
and judging by the loud noises some people still make it still
hasn't – that the louder you shout and the cockier your predictions are, the harder the bump you get when it puts you
on your backside, which almost inevitably it does.

It is history that Manchester United used Wembley that
day to put on an exhibition that left Leicester wondering
what had hit them. Sir Stanley Rous, that mighty man of
FIFA, was moved to say that it was the most academic display he had seen in a Cup Final.

That Cup-winning team comprised: David Gaskell, our
home-bred goalkeeper, Tony Dunne, an Eire nipper I
bought for peanuts from Shelbourne, Noel Cantwell, experienced Eire international, Pat Crerand, Scottish cap and
the most telling long-ball passer in the game, the indestructible England cap Bill Foulkes, the tigerish great-heart

Maurice Setters, little Johnny Giles, an Eire babe from our creche who later was to do such great things for Leeds United so that people with hindsight have ever since said that I gave him away to Leeds in September 1963 for £34,000 (about which more later), England man Albert Quixall, Scottish cap David Herd, with a mighty shot, Denis Law, who scored twenty-three League goals in his first season for us, and the Babe Bobby Charlton, who continued to eat up matches voraciously for England and for United from 1958, the boy who became a man overnight.

In that season 1962-3, others of our own infants learning the trade in the hard school of the First Division included Seamus Brennan (thirty-seven games), who later played for Eire, Jimmy Nicholson (later Northern Ireland), a little snapping whippet called Norbert Stiles (thirty-one games), who with Bobby Charlton was in Sir Alf Ramsey's 1966 World Cup winning England team, and Norbert Lawton, later to skipper Preston North End at Wembley (playing for them alongside another of our babes, Alex Dawson).

So our nursery, born of old, old yearning to bring up my new boys, was again proving priceless.

New signings, big signings are sometimes invaluable and inevitable. But for depth, for immediate replacement in emergency, only a piece that fits the pattern will do. The pieces that usually fit best are those you have carved yourself, to your own design.

Unluckily the production line from a nursery cannot be constant or consistent. Because these are human, not inanimate pieces. There are boom years and there are lean years, as we had seen and as we shall see. But that does not mean that the search for youth can be given up. It must never be given up.

We had more expensive 'immigrants' in the United team than at any other time under my managership. But that was because we lost too much quality at one disastrous blow, most of it home grown.

Anyway we had won the Cup, which was good for our ego. We were back in Europe in the Cupwinners' Cup. Our supporters were feeling important again. I had a feeling we were on our way back.

In the next season (1963-4) we finished runners-up in the League, were semi-finalists in the FA Cup and quarter-finalists in the European Cupwinners' Cup, in which after leading 4-1 in the first leg against Sporting Lisbon we crashed out 5-0 in the second.

In September 1963 Johnny Giles was transferred to Leeds United for a fee of £34,000. Here is why:

I had left him out of the team. He had played ninety-nine League games and scored ten League goals for Manchester United, having joined us as a boy. And he played in the previous season's winning Cup Final against Leicester City. I never had any doubt about his ability and his promise. Yet I still felt he was not quite mature enough, and that is the reason why I left him out of the side. The fact that I brought in younger players from time to time was not the point. It was his maturity that I was concerned about. He obviously felt differently. He did not want to play in the Central League team. So in keeping with my insistence that we would not keep an unhappy player, I made him available for transfer.

He did mature eventually with Leeds, and he is certainly a tougher character than he was when he was at Old Trafford. And these qualities have made him the very good player he now is at Elland Road.

But when I am asked am I sorry I let him go (asked, as I have said before, with hindsight) I invite questioners to examine our record since, and say: 'How can I be sorry?'

Anyway, since I have never allowed directors to pick my teams for me I was not prepared to let a player pick them. If I had they would all want to pick teams, because every professional wants to be in the first team. I don't blame them, but if they didn't want to play in the team I picked them for I didn't want them to play for me at all.

Another tiddler, Nobby Stiles, who made his senior debut in October 1960, was prepared to wait to be fully established until I thought he was good and ready, though I knew he sometimes thought he should have been in when he wasn't. But when his real chance came little Nobby took it with both hands, both legs, his big heart and his chattering, nattering, nagging, urging, admonishing, inspiring mouth, not to mention making the most of the inferior eyesight he had been handicapped with.

It did not matter who was captain, Nobby had more to say than anybody else in any match. He would give everybody, anybody a fearful rollicking who lapsed even momentarily from two hundred per cent effort, which was his own minimum. If we were winning he would exhort us not to let up, but his great value was that he was *compelling*. He raised us when we flagged.

Set Nobby Stiles a job and he would do it if it killed him. No opponent was too big for this bantam, physically or by repute. Jimmy Greaves, Eusebio, or anybody else, none of them scared Nobby, as brave a little football warrior as ever trod a pitch. I always admired Sir Alf Ramsey for sticking by Nobby Stiles. I knew the lad's value to a team. A team is far the better for his type but there are not many like him. Nobby well repaid Sir Alf.

I do not have to be told that Nobby's occasional excess of enthusiasm had him in conflict with referees, or that he was a player opposing supporters were inclined to give a bit of stick to. But I shall never be persuaded that Nobby Stiles was a dirty player and I never saw a player badly injured by him, though I concede he might have bruised a few. And he has a bruise or two to show for it. If he overdid it I would say to him after the match: 'What are you doing, you silly lad, getting yourself in trouble?' and he might say: 'I'm sorry. I was daft. I shouldn't have done it.'

In that same 1963-4 season, another tiddler emerged, a black-haired, short-cropped, insignificant-looking infant of about 9 stone wet through, scarcely out of nursery's nappies. I knew this boy George Best could play. Everybody in the club who watched him knew he could play. The things he could do with a ball first made you blink and then made you wonder. He had a congenital dislike of letting anybody else have a kick at it. The problem was in getting it from him to have a try.

He could do things with either foot that most fellows couldn't do with their better one. What looked deceptively like spindles for legs could hit that ball with a fair whack. But other things even than these have to be there to make a Football League player, let alone a player in the toughest, fastest, keenest competition in the world, the First Division. We knew George's heart was in the right place. He would take the best players on and had no complaint when he was flattened for his cheek in trying to beat one player four times. But, for one thing, would his physique stand up to it

56

all? I went to see him play in a reserve game at Chesterfield. When I came back I said: 'It's time for him to go in.'

But another necessary quality – and one that cannot be measured, anticipated or practised – is temperament. I have known many examples of players who are absolutely wonderful at practice. But come match day and they have left all their wonders in the training ground last Tuesday. The hottest property in a scratch practice match can freeze on the big day in front of the big crowd. Anyway the big day came for the small boy. It was 14 September 1963. How did wee George react? He didn't react at all! The dressing room on match day is a bit edgy. Players are jumping around feigning to do exercises. Some are full of funny patter. Some are fussing with their bootlaces. Some are just fussing.

The boy Best sat in a corner reading the club programme! He was completely unconcerned!

The match began and almost immediately the little whipper-snapper had taken the game by the scruff of the neck and was cheekily beating his man as if he had been in the First Division for ten years.

From the very moment he started to play in the first team, George Best had pulses racing. How opposing crowds felt about him (though I am sure they all admired his great skill, hence the size of the crowds who flocked to see him) was exemplified, I think, in a match we played in Christchurch, New Zealand. George had led the opposition a real old dance and I heard a New Zealander behind me keep saying: 'Oh dear, he's got it again!'

George wasn't interested in the birds (or the bees, I shouldn't think) in those days in 1963. At least if he was it wasn't getting in the papers. The only thing complicated about George then was what he did with the ball. My only thoughts about him were wondering if what I saw when he played was really true or if I was just dreaming. Nightmares were to come later, as we shall see.

PATTERN

What *is* this pattern of playing I keep going on about? Only the naive would imagine that it is a drill to be followed by every Manchester United player. It is a pattern formed by the players on the staff, formed by individuals who are all different, and therefore the pattern over the years will gradually change. But *only* gradually.

What are the basic needs? They are the needs of every club. From the back the need is for a goalkeeper who is in charge in the penalty area, who has an understanding with his colleages by thought reading as well as shouting, as well as having an appreciation of angles and *using* the ball at the right time.

Full-backs require strength, pace, and need to be quick on the turn for recovery purposes – needs that are not new to football but are perhaps even more vital now than they were twenty years ago. All the back men, say four of them, need to have comand in the air, have to be able to read situations before they arise, all along the line.

What is now termed a sweeper has to be a smeller of danger to come, and this was never better done than by Nobby Stiles, who was taking up positions to counter situations when the ball was at the other end of the park. All these defenders, too, must use the ball accurately. The one thing to be avoided is giving the ball away. I know it is impossible not to give it away occasionally, but the team that does it least is the one that wins the prizes.

For real success the middle men, the creators, are the ones who really shape the game, the ones from whom most blessings flow. Deep-lying inside-forwards and wing-halves used to do the job, so there is nothing actually new about middle men, the only difference now being whether the method is to use two mainly or three. Four is a policy of fear. Whatever the method these are the men predominantly who start things. They have to have vision, imagination to hold the ball or pass it if passing it is 'on', and ability to beat a man, which is the hard way, used if a pass that will do the same work for him more swiftly and economically is not on. But the middle man has also to be able to *win* the ball, so he has to be able to tackle, read, or smell when an interception is going to present itself. There have been few more creative middle men in my time than Pat Crerand, a bold, constructive player if ever I saw one.

Forwards must obviously have great skill because they are facing the wrong way half the time when the ball comes to them. They have to be able to take a bump and bounce back. They, too, have to anticipate situations and exploit them. They have to 'lose' opponents by taking up positions that allow it, which is one reason why really great players seem to have more time than lesser men, thus having escaped by anticipating the tight marking, especially the ultra-tight marking of today.

A forward, particularly, has constantly to give himself a view of the pitch before the ball reaches him, thus allowing him a preconceived notion of what he intends to do when he gets it. Compared with twenty years ago, wingers are a rarity, but still most goals come from crosses from the flanks, high, low, or knee-high, so all forwards have to have some of a winger's qualities and so do middle men and even fullbacks for that matter. Then, of course, to provide the finish to the whole operation, the need is for two or three of those priceless characters who have the knack of putting the ball into the net, and of whom Manchester United have had more than their share, like Stan Pearson, Jack Rowley, Billy Whelan, Denis Violett, Tommy Taylor, Bobby Charlton, Denis Law, David Herd and George Best among others.

A bonus, if a team contains all those assets, is the genius in the ranks. United have had a few of these. These fellows are by nature nonconformists, inasmuch as they do things that the others cannot do. I have always believed that the brilliant individualist must be given scope for his nonconformism as long as it is not at the expense of the end product – the scoring of goals. Because the constant surprises inflicted on the opposition by these gifted players become confidence-sapping for them, making them disbelieve in themselves. For various reasons, among United forwards, I would put Jack Rowley, Billy Whelan, Bobby Charlton, Denis Law and George Best, at least in this category.

The great Real Madrid had all these qualities plus the vital and often missing link, complete understanding, and it was this I was aiming for when first I began managing Manchester United. It is the *understanding* that makes the pattern from the individuals in it.

To create it the first job is making a player aware of what his own position demands, whether it is destructive, creative, or both, what he is required to do in any situation. All players do things differently, even if only slightly differently.

But basic requirements are the same, and knowing the requirements laid down for offensive or defensive situations, they are given constant practice in them. Since the reserves and other young players also often take part in the practice, the pattern is constantly being formed throughout the club, varied, as I said, only slightly and gradually as the odd player finishes or moves on whose individual style has affected the pattern and has been affected by it.

Thus also not only has a player learned the requirements and practised them, he has learned from sheer practice the requirements of his colleagues, and the idiosyncrasies of his colleagues (and they all have them) until they become a team of thought-readers.

I was sometimes accused, or Manchester United were accused of 'playing it off the cuff' when some other teams with lesser talents regimented themselves into becoming boring, defensive, mechanical morons.

But if the care with which we of Manchester United created our pattern, which was adapted to change with changes of individuals, and which was torn to shreds at Munich, and then created again, if all this is playing it off the cuff my critics know more about the game than I do. And this being football they are perfectly entitled to think they do. But results speak louder than words in football. Ours in the Sixties bear inspection.

I *did* resist, and I am not ashamed to say so, the temptation to make Manchester United's game as boring as most teams played it, with this plague of a plan to go away and try to draw 0-0 (going out not to lose instead of going out to win) and to use what they comically called four-three-three when really it was five-four-one. Our attendances were evidence of what the public thought about our 'off-the-cuff' methods.

Real Madrid, the splendid Tottenham Hotspur team with Danny Blanchflower and Dave Mackay, *three* Manchester United teams in two decades, these were the teams with pattern in their play, with something to show worth watching. Look what defensive rubbish did to Italian football! It nearly killed it, and for all it was worth as a no-goal

60

spectacle it would have been good riddance, but luckily the Italians seem to have seen the light and the true value of their brilliant performers will be seen again.

Critics of Manchester United's venturesome football in the Sixties should reflect as I often do on how good the second of our great sides, the Busby Babes, would have become. It took Leeds United under Don Revie several years to reach their own peak. The Babes, as babes, won two championships.

My young team never got within several years of maturity before they were torn from us. Goodness knows what peak they would have reached. And I could have sat back for at least five years knowing that they would become better and better and I need only have worried about, and indeed could have concentrated upon the next lot of Babes emerging. As emerging they were.

In the season 1963-4, having won the Cup the previous season and having finished a deceptively low nineteenth in the First Division, we reached the third of our *five FA Cup semi-finals in succession* and finished runners-up in the League. The following 'home-grown' players appeared in League matches in that season: Anderson (two games), Best (seventeen), Brennan (seventeen), Charlton (forty), Chisnall (twenty), Dunne (forty), Foulkes (forty-one), Gaskell (seventeen), Moir (eighteen), Sadler (nineteen), Stiles (seventeen), Tranter (one).

And the next season (1964-5) we won the championship! So in 1965-6 we were in the 'big one', the European Cup again.

During that bad League season of 1962-3, when we won the Cup and finished fourth from the bottom, Jimmy Murphy and I had discussed the situation, point by point, player by player, result by result. What must we alter if anything? What was going wrong? We decided that what we were doing was right, on the right lines anyway, and that results were bound to come if we maintained even slight progress.

The play was good enough except for the finish and the luck, and we were not by nature a couple of fellows who take bad luck as an excuse. The Cup win was the best confirmation we could have had. I also told the players as I had constantly told them, that if they kept on playing football, that is football the United way, the results would be bound to follow sooner rather than later.

Jimmy and I had decided that we could see we were about to climb the staircase. Well, now we had climbed it to the Championship, which was the ceiling, in only two more seasons, and were about to reach for the sky, the European Cup.

We disposed of Helsinki in the preliminary round by an aggregate of 9-2 over the two legs, and then A.S.K. Vorwaerts of East Berlin by 5-1 in the first round. Then came the real test, against Benfica of Lisbon, twice winners of the trophy, first leg at Old Trafford, in the quarter-final.

We managed to win 3-2 at Old Trafford. But a single-goal lead to take away to Lisbon was not calculated to fill us with excess optimism. Our players have never underestimated themselves. After all, though Benfica had the wonderful Eusebio, 'the Black Panther' with a kick like a donkey, and others who would be top class in my league, our forward line did not read too badly – Best, Law, Charlton, Herd, Connelly, internationals all.

But a single goal start was little enough advantage with 75,000 Portuguese screaming their Latin heads off.

George Best was so overawed by all this that he shut them up altogether. El Beatle he might have looked to them, but Benfica, who had to chase in his bewildering wake, doubtless wished he had never been born. In fact the whole United team so eclipsed their mighty hosts that we beat them 5-1, winning on aggregate by the astonishing margin of 8-3.

So we were entitled to feel that on our way to the sky, we had at least got through one fairly high cloud. But football is the greatest deflater I know. First you feel full of puff. Next you are popped. It happens so often that I cannot understand people in the game who make predictions, or sometimes who even merely express opinions. It will be noticed that the spectator (or anybody else) who shouts loudest inevitably and immediately is made to look the most idiotic.

Well, we did not make loud noises of confidence. But we reasonably had great hopes. After all, what we had done to Benfica surely we could repeat, if not by the same margin, against Partizan of Belgrade. That is what we felt, anyway.

But what *did* happen was that Partizan won 2-0 in Belgrade and we won by only 1-0 at Old Trafford, and that one goal in their favour was more useful by far than most of the goals we scored against Benfica.

By then I had reached the stage of thinking we were not meant to win this competition. I could well understand Don Revie's feelings when Leeds United seemed always to be the bridesmaid and never the blushing bride even in home competitions. I sympathized from many experiences. I do not say that being nearly champions or nearly Cupwinners is worse than being relegated. But an astonishing thing about football is that a near-misser is an unhappy man. He can win nearly everything and be ready to burst into tears. I have heard unsuccessful managers saying : 'I wish I had his bad luck,' in talking about a runner-up. And I agree. There is little satisfying about mediocrity, even safe mediocrity. Anyway in that 1965-6 season we lost two semi-finals in a week!

So I was gloomy after being beaten by Partizan, who, incidentally, lost to Real Madrid in the Final. But Pat Crerand heard me say the prize didn't seem to be meant for us and he pooh-poohed me. 'We'll win it, believe me,' he said.

And somehow I felt better. Crerand was good for morale.

We were fourth in the League that season and the next season (1966-7) we were champions again. So once again the European Cup was there to be won. There it was, high in the sky shining at us, twinkling like a star, almost beckoning us.

On aggregate were dismissed Hibernian (Malta) 4-0, Sarajevo 2-1, Gornik 2-1 (after 105,000 people had seen us lose 1-0 in Silesia) and then in the semi-final we bumped into our old friends Real Madrid. The best we could do against them at Old Trafford was to win 1-0, and that obviously couldn't go to our heads. In fact before we knew where we were in the return in Madrid we had conceded three goals to one by us. I was sick as I found my way to the dressing room at half-time. The players had their heads between their legs. So I put it to them very strongly that we were really only one goal down on aggregate. Things had not gone well, I said, but there were forty-five minutes more. So we must be venturesome. We could not win if we were not venturesome, and it would not make any difference if we lost by more goals than the one we were behind if we lost at all. So we must not fear defeat. We must go at them.

And we were transformed. David Sadler made it 3-3 on aggregate, and then George Best stuck a chance on for, of all people, that great defensive destroyer Bill Foulkes.

With 100,000 apprehensive Spaniards watching, the sight of Big Bill tearing down the pitch and then connecting with George Best's cross will be a memory I shall cherish to the end of my days. That, indeed, was going at them!

Manchester City beat us in the run-in to the Championship but that disappointment was countered by prospects of the big thing to come. We were on the last rung of the staircase to the sky. On 29 May at Wembley we were to meet Benfica, Eusebio and all, in the Final of the European Cup.

THE EUROPEAN CUP

Managing a top-class football club is not like managing any other business. As long as the machines in a factory are maintained efficiently those machines, barring rare accidents, will do the job. And, except during epidemics, employee casualties are rare, so that the machines are practically always fully manned.

With a football team all a manager's real assets, his players, do a job that brings them up against opponents in situations of constant tension and physical strain, so that accidents are happening all the time. Seldom if ever are all a club's players fully fit. And the great players are as vulnerable as the ordinary player, the greatest of them even more so because their skill with the ball is utilised so late against an opponent's tackle and by so small a margin of space that an inaccurate but innocent bid for the ball becomes a kick on the ankle for the great one. Skill is utilised so late because the later it operates the less chance the tackler has to recover in time to tackle again. In other words the great man puts himself in the greatest danger in order to create the greatest danger to opposition.

Another problem the normal business or factory manager doesn't have to face is that of fan worship of his employees. Even show business stars are not subjected to the perpetual attentions of top-class footballers, who scarcely have a private life to call their own. This, of course, is especially true before big games.

Successful footballers have a million friends, which include a handful of real friends and 900,000 hangers on. Or perhaps it only seems like 900,000. That a footballer when eventually he retires finds he has only the handful of friends is no matter. He has the 900,000 as permanent satellites while he is in the firmament.

I do not refer to the supporters, who merely pass him a spot of banter, the humour of which varies with his hits or misses of the previous Saturday. A player laps these up as he patiently signs autographs in mid-meal, or for the same small boy who has had the same autograph umpteen times before. As dear old Frank Swift used to say: 'The time I'll begin to worry is when they don't ask me.'

Anyway all the fuss is not the best preparation for a big game. I know there is a school of thought that criticizes the idea of taking players away from home to prepare for games or even to escape, giving as the reason a player's preference for his wife's or his mother's cooking, and home comforts, over days in an impersonal hotel.

There is something to be said for this, of course, but when a player cannot stir out of his house without being beseiged by people, even people with the kindest possible motives, there is nothing for it but to look for an escape.

Of course I would have preferred to keep them at home and within a short distance of our modern training and treatment facilities. One of the great burdens of professional football is the welter of travelling and the bore of living in even the best hotels. Nor does any happily married young fellow enjoy leaving home for a weekend with his workmates, no matter how he admires them. Who doesn't want to get away from his mates at the end of a working day?

But there are advantages. It really is necesary to move players out of their environment and its fan pressures from time to time. I decided that in the days leading up to a European Cup Final it was essential.

So I took them to Egham, Surrey, for peace and quiet. And there I reflected, in between worrying whether anybody had toothache, or any other ache, whether anybody would fall over a matchstick, what we would do today and the next day, and whether little Nobby Stiles's calf would repair in time, since it had caused him to miss an England game. And principally I cogitated on the absence of one of our greatest assets.

Because Denis Law, that destroyer of opposition with his lightning reflexes and overhead-kicked goals, who would snap up unconsidered trifles and stick them in the net, was at that moment recovering from an operation to a knee that had created havoc with him that season, culminating in his missing the semi-final second leg in Madrid.

So no Denis Law and no Championship, which we seemed to have won until Manchester City came along and beat us to it. This was not the happiest pair of preludes for a test against Benfica, who had been in the European Cup Final four times, won it twice, and had not only the Black Panther Eusebio still electrifying watchers with his shooting, but other such majestic figures as their skipper, Mario Coluna, who wielded tremendous influence on the team, the slippery Simoes, and the elongated Jose Torres, who wreaked havoc on opposing defences from his dizzy height of about 6ft 4in.

But after all, we had a few aces of our own.

Meanwhile, our chairman, Louis Edwards, and I, had watched the Lisbon leg of Benfica's semi-final against Juventus. It might be thought that this was a good excuse for a pleasant trip to a pleasant place. Only those in football, or who have as much travelling to do as people in the football game, realize that *any* travelling is a chore.

But we *had* thrashed Benfica not so long before, so what new was there to find out? Well for one thing, in a European Cup semi-final the best teams are fielded wherever possible and those best players are doing precisely as they would be doing in the final if they got there and that is going all out, according to their pattern, and that pattern could have changed if ever so slightly. We wanted to know.

Never was a trip more worthwhile.

Benfica had all their usual skills and power, but, much to my surprise, I noticed that their right full-back, who was quite happy and competent when the ball came to him, was very slow on the turn. So in my talks to the players at Egham I was able to stress that John Aston, left-winger, son of John our old international, should take advantage of this. Young John must not take the ball to the full-back. He must put it past him and run. I would not be concerned if in trying to do so he lost the ball down our left flank at their end, as long as he follows my orders to hit the ball and go.

Nobby Stiles would be required, not for the first time in his life, to attend to the great Eusebio. Bill Foulkes would counter the air-raids of Torres. Every contingency was prepared for. And we would aim to dominate the middle of the pitch.

Summing it all up at Wembley before the game I did as I always do at Wembley. I impressed upon them all the disastrous consequences of losing concentration and giving the ball away aimlessly. The chasing this causes can be destroying. It saps energy and plays havoc with morale. Wembley is a place for real football, and that means accurate passing that keeps the ball and preserves confidence and energy.

Then they were on the pitch, amidst an almost unbelievable atmosphere of expectation. At least 95,000 of the 100,000, patently on our side, seemed to be throwing out vibrations willing us to win. We, the generals, with our plans and our talks, were done with it, for forty-five minutes at any rate. And what are generals without good fighting troops? The best laid schemes gang more aft agley for footballers than for mice and poets. A shot or a pass only a blade of grass out on impact can be a foot awry where that foot is calamitous. Was this to be yet another disappointment, just ten years after the hideous day of Munich, the wrenching from us of a young team not yet mature but so magnificent that I am sure the 1958 European Cup would have been ours, and after it, ours and ours and ours again?

Both sides soon began to create good situations with highly skilled movements, but, as I had hoped – and have always aimed at with my teams – we got a grip on the middle, the real hub of affairs, where loose balls are apt to go and whence those splendid pickers up of morsels, what we used to call wing-halves and inside-forwards, create moves of simplicity and devastation.

John Aston carried out his task to the letter and played the game of his life, subjecting the hapless full-back to a nightmare he was doubtles relieved to waken from at the end.

But it was not until the fifty-third minute that David Sadler sent over a ball to which Bobby Charlton leapt and directed it beautifully into the net with his head. I thought the blast from 95,000 throats would knock the house down. But then we lost control in the middle slightly and, at what might have been a morale-destroying time for us, only twelve minutes from the end of normal time, Benfica made the score 1-1 when, for once, Torres escaped from Foulkes and won a high one, heading on to Graca who scored from only about five yards. Woe, woe, woe. I could have wept. But I could have leapt only a few moments before the end of ninety minutes when Eusebio put in a shot that would surely have gone straight through the net to goodness knows where except for one of the greatest saves it has ever been my relief to see.

Alex Stepney not only stopped it. He held it! If there had ever been any doubt in my mind about the wisdom of paying Chelsea £52,000 for him in September 1966, which there had not, it would have been dispelled for ever there and then.

Incidentally, that was one of the few moments during which Eusebio eluded that little lad who was all man, Nobby Stiles, and I have always since maintained that if Eusebio had placed the ball better instead of trying to burst the net with it we should probably not have survived the normal time.

I talked to the tired, leg-weary players as they sat or lay on the turf for a few minutes before going into extra time, and once again I stressed my old maxim that we must regain the middle of the park. From the kick-off this is exactly what we did. Only two minutes went before Stepney sent a clearance down the pitch and Brian Kidd headed it on to George Best. And I can still see George going past opponents, including the goalkeeper, and placing the ball calmly in the net as if he had been on a croft playing with a rubber ball. No wonder Pat Crerand took him in his arms and showed him to the crowd.

The noise, if possible, was even more deafening than before. I believe the crowd now sensed that we had them and that the extra minutes, far from giving confidence to Benfica who had so nearly won, were going to knock the stuffing out of them. And sure enough, only minutes later Brian Kidd celebrated his nineteenth birthday by showing his reflexes were razor sharp when he first headed the ball against Henrique's body and then headed the rebound into the net.

It remain only for Bobby Charlton to score a symbolic goal with a superb flick of the ball to flatten Benfica completely. It could not have been scored by a more fitting scorer.

For an infinitesimal blank in time I did not realize what had happened. Then the blast in what seemed millions of decibels hit me. We had won but it seemed to have come so suddenly after the years of waiting. Half an hour ago we were on the knife-edge. What a difference thirty little minutes can make! I had a brief thought about Benfica, so near and yet so far. It lasted about three seconds, and then emotion set in. I was among the boys, the Cup was ours at last, there were tears all round, Bobby Charlton and Pat Crerand went straight to bed with churned-up-tummy trouble instead of going daft with the rest of us at the banquet, Denis Law switched off his television set from his bed in a Manchester hospital and slept with a big smile on his face, and the crowd joined what appeared to be the rest of the entire population of Britain in rejoicing.

To show what a whirl my mind was in at the banquet, I became one of the few Scotsmen in history to lose a lot of money and not know it. I had won the Manager of the Year award and had been presented with a cheque for £1,000. During the celebrations someone came along to me and said: 'I think this belongs to you.' It was my cheque for £1,000 which, grossly outraging my birthright, I had carelessly dropped to the floor.

In winning the European Cup Final 4-1 against magnificent Benfica we fielded the following team: Stepney; Brennan, Dunne; Crerand, Foulkes, Stiles; Best, Kidd, Charlton, Sadler, Aston.

Of these, eight were from Manchester United's own creche, including the entire forward line, if I include David Sadler, signed for £750 from Maidstone on his seventeenth birthday. And Dunne cost practically nothing. I felt that not only had I, personally, fulfilled my great ambition by helping Manchester United win the European Cup, but that also those eight players were further evidence that my original dreams even before I became a manager twenty-two years earlier, dreams of my own nursery for footballers, had come true again. As I may say, with apologies to greater singers (though I am not bad with 'Jeannie with the light-brown hair'), I had done it my way.

It takes a great team to win the European Cup. It was my third great team in more than a score of years. Others created one great team; rare ones, like Bill Shankly at Liverpool, two great teams. I am grateful to have been blessed with the energy to survive the strain of creating three. It could not have been done merely by gaining respect. To respect must be added affection – mutual affection. That's what we at Manchester United had.

Amidst the elation at the banquet that night, it was chastening to see Jackie Blanchflower and Johnny Berry among the guests. Both had survived our Munich tragedy. Neither played football again, cut off from their profession in their very prime, an awful reminder of our perilous journey up the staircase to the sky.

THE WILD ONES

With the European Cup won, there remained only one competition to win. It was an unofficial championship, dubbed the World Cup Championship, between the champions of Europe and the champions of South America. There were people who thought we should avoid it. These matches had a habit of becoming battles if not wars.

The year before, in 1967, Celtic had beaten Racing Club of Argentina 1-0 at Hampden, but even before the second leg in Buenos Aires kicked off, Celtic's goalkeeper was hit by a missile and couldn't play. And the play-off in Montevideo was a sheer rough-house in which four Celtic players and two Racing players were sent off.

In the 1966 World Cup even the phlegmatic Sir Alf Ramsey had described the Argentinians as animals.

But football is a world game and I do not think that a problem can be solved by running away from it. Anyway we took it on, and I think one of the troubles was that we felt the aftermath.

First our chairman, Louis Edwards, and I went over to

see our opponents, Estudiantes, play in Buenos Aires. The Estudiantes people could not have been more hospitable, but when we arrived with the team in September 1968 we had the feeling that things were hotting up. The world hoped for a sporting contest and for lessons to have been learned from the Celtic fiasco.

First our party, players and all, were invited to a cocktail party two evenings before the game, at the Boca Juniors stadium, where the first leg was to be played. Cocktail parties are not the sort of preparation we care for before matches, but as a gesture of goodwill we said we would go along for an hour. Our players would be able to get together with theirs and this could help, perhaps, when they got out on to the park to play. Not a single Estudiantes player arrived at the cocktail party. We did not stay long.

A Benfica coach did not help when, having been invited to write a piece for the Estudiantes-United match programme, he incensed the local population by condemning Nobby Stiles out of hand.

The shambles of a match almost defies description. We were subjected to series of acts of intimidation, aggravation and provocation that prevented us from even approaching our best football against a team we would have beaten hands down for football skills.

Sir Alf called the Argentinians animals for their antics in a match in England. Estudiantes were at home in the Argentine, with even fewer inhibitions and roared on by their own supporters. Stiles mopped blood from an eyebrow, having been butted and spat at. Francis Burns was felled by Togneri, who, warned by the referee, ran back and punched George Best who was in the middle of the field nowhere near the Burns' incident. Bobby Charlton was carried off to have four stitches in a gash on the shin. A linesman, who seemed to run the game more than the referee, pushed Best in the chest.

Bobby Charlton, normally uncomplaining, said: 'When you have been knocked down, one of them will come to help you. It looks very friendly but it doesn't feel it when you are seized by the skin round your armpits and dragged to your feet.' There was hair-pulling in pretence for ruffling it, elbowing, and every trick in their book. And Sir Stanley

Rous was quoted thus: 'The most remarkable feature was the quite remarkable tolerance of the United players.'

Ultimately, eleven minutes from the end, poor little Nobby Stiles was sent off, after all the provocation he had suffered, for disagreeing with an offside decision and apparently gesticulating at a linesman.

We lost 1-0.

Then, of course, we worried from that day how our crowd would react when Estudiantes visited us in October. As it turned out the only things they threw, as far as I am aware, were words. The match at Old Trafford was no showpiece. George Best and their Hugo Medina were sent off for fighting. Estudiantes' Veron (fouling), Bilardo and Echobar (arguing) were booked, and Denis Law was carried off to be stitched up after colliding with their goalkeeper.

Veron scored a quick goal that 'killed' us, I think. Willie Morgan scored for us late on and Brian Kidd had the ball in the net but although television showed the ball over the line, the referee did not allow it. So we lost on aggregate 2-1.

Overall the whole two-match performance did nothing to enhance the dreary reputation of the World Cup Championship, and we got little more than bruises out of it. Yet I still think we were right to go for this prize. It is up to the football legislators to keep football clean. I know it is the players who do the kicking. They will confine their kicking to the ball if it is made too expensive for them to do otherwise. So it is national bodies who will have to get together and forget nationalism in a determined bid to make football all over the world a safe game to play again.

I stressed to my players throughout my managerial career that they should not allow aggravations to provoke them into retaliation. And I have played merry hell with them when they have retaliated. But there are limits to what a man can stand. It is against the law to kick a man whether he is on the street or on a football pitch. It would be a wonderfully Christian chap who, kicked on the ankle as he was waiting for a bus, would give the assailant his other leg to kick or even go so far as to say: 'I say old chap. I didn't like that. It was rather painful.'

Nine men out of ten would kick or punch back, though psychiatrists would doubtless feel sorrier for the assailant than the victim on account of his having been frustrated when he was an infant delinquent.

But whatever a psychiatrist said to a footballer, that footballer, subjected to a vendetta of hacking, pinching or punching by an opponent, would be bound to reach the state wherein he just could not stand any more of it and take a poke back. So he goes in the book or is sent off, side by side with the villain who provoked him. I await with some impatience for a referee to forget the words of the law in dealing with the victim, use instead the spirit of the law, send off the assailant, leave the victim to play on and thereby teach the assailant the error of his ways.

UNDER NEW MANAGEMENT

At the beginning of 1969, after twenty-three years of my self-demanded role as Managing Manager of Manchester United, I decided I had to unload the playing side of it all to a younger man. I had had enough. It was always a demanding task. I would not have had it any other way. But Manchester United had become not just a football club. It had become a world-famous organization, and the demands had grown every year from the start until it had reached far beyond the power, the energy or the capacity of one man to do. I could hardly see over the top of the pile of correspondence on my desk every morning.

A football club manager has to be with his players every morning if he is going to be in any position to pick teams, weigh up young hopefuls, talk to coaches, trainers, physiotherapists, young arrivals, parents, and properly attend to everything within the orbit of the part of the club that matters most, the performance of the team. We are proud of the splendid stadium at Old Trafford, which we have built from the war-wrecked ruin since 1946. But none of this would have been possible without success on the pitch, from which, in any football club, all blessings fall. The demands became so great that I just could not spend enough time with the players.

So I decided, entirely of my own volition, to shed the load, to hand over the playing side to a younger man.

Mr Louis Edwards, the chairman, and his board, did not see it this way at all. They would much prefer me to carry on, they said. But I had made up my mind. So the problem of my replacement as team manager loomed. And problem it was. Because for a start it was clear that any new man we appointed would, as I had done twenty-three years before, demand his own choice of staff. This would mean that loyal servants who had achieved so much with young and established players might be affected.

Servants like my friend and aide Jimmy Murphy, who had been through so much joy and agony with me, Jack Crompton, our trainer coach, Wilf McGuinness, who had shown great qualities in coaching young players – so much so that he was coach of the England Under-23 team under Sir Alf Ramsey – Johnny Aston, another of our coaches, Joe Armstrong, still a great scout if near the end of the road, and others. All these had virtually lived with me, or they had spent at least as much time with me as ever football had allowed me to spend at home.

With this in mind, and possibly in the hope that the pattern and continuity I had always tried to preserve would be so preserved, the board agreed with my recommendation to give a chance to Wilf McGuinness who, young as he was, had made his way as a coach and had been with the club straight from school. He would be chief coach, with the prospect later of becoming team manager. I would be general manager. This was in April 1969.

People may say it was a mistake to be *too* loyal. I do not know what is meant by being *too* loyal. A man is loyal or he is not. Loyalty is responding to loyalty in kind. Loyalty is also, I think, being human. I should have been less than human had I not been concerned about Manchester United's loyal servants.

From my loyal servants I chose McGuinness. As it turned out, and certainly not because of any question of loyalty, it was a mistake. The fact that Wilf was suddenly put in charge of his own contemporaries as players may well have contributed to it. Young soldiers promoted to lance-corporal in their own platoons sometimes found it embarrassing. I do not even say Wilf found it embarrassing. He was a lively character, not short of a line of patter, who was good enough a coach to be in charge of England's

Under-23s. But for one reason or another, whether inexperience or slight immaturity, which is almost the same thing, he did not get the response I had hoped he would get from the players. If he and the players did not quite 'gel' I do not think for a minute it was deliberate on either side. Indeed, Manchester United reached three semi-finals under Wilf, so it cannot be said that he had not achieved some success. But I felt when we reached fifth from the bottom of the First Division by December 1970 that, at the board's request, I should step in and try to do something about it myself. It had been a trial period of twenty months for Wilf.

What would have happened if we had beaten Leeds United in our FA Cup thrice-played semi-final under Wilf, as we were unlucky not to do in two of the three games at least, and then gone on to win the Final at Wembley, I would not care to speculate on.

I can assure my doubters that I did *not* want to take the team reins again. I must reassert that I did *not* interfere with Wilf McGuinness's team job in any way. For example, I did not agree with Wilf's dropping Bobby Charlton and Denis Law on the same day, as he did on one occasion. I do not wish to say that I would not have dropped Bobby or Denis or anybody else if I thought it was the right thing to do. I did not think it was the right time to do it. But I kept my opinion to myself. Possibly he did it to make a point, if so I still did not think that day was the day to do it if he *had* to do it. But if I had contemplated going back on my word and interfering with Wilf's team selection that would certainly have roused me to do so. I did not interfere then or ever.

Wilf McGuinness was offered his old job, but eventually he left and took a coaching job in Greece. I do not blame him for taking this course. I still think he has a lot to offer football, and, like all my old players and staff who have gone elsewhere, I genuinely wish him well.

At board meetings Wilf was confident enough. He made his points and most were accepted. Nobody has all his points accepted at any meetings. If they were there would not be a point in having meetings. He asked my advice at least once. We had been through one unhappy spell of non-success and he came to me one day and said: 'What team would you play on Saturday?' I gave him my team and he selected it. We went to Wolves and made a draw and did not lose for ten matches. I would not have complained if he had not selected my chosen team.

Wilf's mistakes, I repeat in my opinion, were in his handling of players he had been brought up with. It is my opinion, too, that he was then too inexperienced to handle them and get full response.

I made an inauspicious restart by losing to Middlesbrough in the third round of the FA Cup after a replay, then we shot up the League table and even had hopes of getting into Europe again, but it was too late and we finished a respectable eighth.

Then we went on tour to Austria and Switzerland and when we were coming away from Zurich, Bobby Charlton, the captain, came to me and said: 'The boys and I have been having a long talk and we want you to know that we would all be very happy if you carried on.' I was very touched by this and I said: 'Bobby, this is one of the nicest things that ever happened to me and I am very grateful, but I've had enough.'

We had improved. We had begun to look a bit more like Manchester United. But I have to admit that little cracks were showing. After nearly a quarter of a century, except for the team's brief spell under Wilf McGuinness, I felt once again that a younger man was needed, a blow of fresh air in the team, and new ideas to give it new life. I have never been one to dwell on and eulogize the past and to criticize the present. I do not like everything the progress of football over the years has brought in its wake. But I do know that if you stand still you are sunk.

UNITED IN CRISIS

So the hunt was on again. And the guessing game. Applicants, as usual when managerships become available, included every type from bricklayers to mathematicians, who claim to have solved the riddle of the football universe, because every football fan is a football manager at heart.

We were looking for someone special, a technical expert, psychologist, driver, humanist and leader, who also had the dignity required of a club held in esteem in all parts of the football world.

It is one thing choosing the man you would like and quite another getting him or even speaking to him. Our friends in the Press, and not unreasonably, pointed out those who would seem to fill our bill and some who would not. Lined up side by side they would have stretched from one goal-mouth to the half-way line.

I propose not to mention any of the names we even contemplated. There is no point in embarrassing them and I would not betray a confidence in this regard anyway. Two well-known managers we negotiated with, but unsuccessfully. It is one thing wanting a manager to join you and quite another to find one available.

One man who had been recommended to us and who had led his team to the FA Cup Final, gone down with them into the Second Division and soon brought them back up again, was Frank O'Farrell. Here was one who might soon be available to negotiate with us.

It had been reported that Frank O'Farrell was due for another contract with Leicester City. Our chairman Louis Edwards, spoke to Leicester's Len Shipman, who was also President of the Football League, and asked if his club would object to our approaching O'Farrell. Mr Shipman took the request to his board and in the end they agreed. I saw Frank O'Farrell and made the initial approach about his joining Manchester United, and he seemed very happy with it. I then arranged for our chairman, Mr Edwards, to see him and confirm details of his contract. And so it was all tied up.

So we had a new manager. And a tremendous responsibility it was. Because Manchester United had been winning things for so long that we were expected to win things all the time. This was not just a team, not just a club, but a legend all over the world, as a glimpse at my still massive postbag confirmed. I could not foresee the future. I did not know whether Frank O'Farrell would bring success to the team. But obviously we thought he could. One could only wait and see.

Frank O'Farrell brought Malcolm Musgrove as his aide and coach, as I had brought Jimmy Murphy. I resolved once more that I would not interfere with team affairs in any way. To make sure that this would not only be so but would be *seen* to be so to any doubters who might turn up to see if I was pushing my nose in, I would not even go to the training ground.

Most days I was at Old Trafford. I was available to help Frank O'Farrell in any way if he thought he needed my advice. I was also there to deal with my still heavy volume of correspondence.

In 1965 the directors in their generosity had decided to make five hundred of the club's shares available to me, and the chairman, Mr Louis Edwards, was quoted as saying: 'We cannot imagine Manchester United without Matt Busby.' It was a quite extraordinary tribute, a gesture to ensure that I would have my share in the club virtually in perpetuity. Eventually I accepted, and was equally grateful when, having handed over the playing affairs of the club to Frank O'Farrell, I was taken on to the board. Thus I had been a professional player with Manchester City, Liverpool and Scotland, manager of Manchester United and Scotland, and was now an amateur director of Manchester United, because directors of Football League clubs are really amateurs since no directors' fees are permitted. In all this my record is probably unique.

Simultaneously, having in my time taken some stick from critics as a player and as a manager, I laid myself wide open to taking a bit more as a director. It must have been the masochist in me. Moreover, having always had quite decided ideas on how directors should behave, and having had, as the reader is by now well aware, forthright ideas about good directors and bad ones, I had laid down my own rules to which I must conform or scrap the first several chapters of this book and try to forget what I had always insisted on.

Nobody could have had more kindness heaped upon him by football enthusiasts all over the world than I have had. I am thankful to them all. I am also well aware that there were those among them who would say it was all Matt Busby's fault when things went wrong at United when I was manager, perhaps because I had not signed almost every player who ever become available for transfer between 1945 and 1969, or because I had not made my team play four-two-four, or four-three-three, or four-four-two or four-six-none, or had not made loud noises in public when a player transgressed, or some such.

I have no doubt that my directorship did not end all that. I have no doubt that lots of things have been all my fault since then, according to the knowing ones we all know, who are to be heard above all others in any conversation (the louder the dafter I always think), and I suppose it is all my fault that they will still say something is all my fault because I insisted on having my own way for so long. Anyway at the risk of sounding like a broken record I say again, if it had anything to do with the playing side it was all Frank O'Farrell's fault and he should be given all the blame (or all the praise). If it was the board's fault, count me in for my share of the blame.

Except for an initial embarrassment in losing to Halifax Town in a Watney Cup match, everything went swimmingly for Manchester United and Frank O'Farrell and Malcolm Musgrove, who could scarcely have had a happier start. By December we were on top by five points. Then came a terrible decline and after three draws we lost seven matches in succession. The disappointments went on to the end of the season.

In the meantime Frank O'Farrell had bought Martin Buchan, a young player of international class from Aberdeen and Ian Moore, fast-raiding, goal-scoring winger, from Nottingham Forest.

Back to that first half of the season. By December George Best had scored fourteen goals and Denis Law twelve, but from then on it was evident to everybody that all was not well with Best. His way of life has always been well reported, of course, but he seemed to have lost his enthusiasm for the game. This disenchantment came as a surprise to me, because at the time of his earlier indiscretions under my management his love for the game and enthusiasm for training had always shone through. George, in fact, was a tremendous trainer.

Then the storm broke. On the eve of the home international series he first announced that he had retired and next arrived in Marbella on the Spanish coast, failed to turn up for Northern Ireland, and later failed to turn up for Manchester United in Tel Aviv.

After his sojourn in the sun he arrived back in

Manchester, was interviewed by Frank O'Farrell, and said he would come back to play for Manchester United.

But all the blame for United's decline in that second half of the season must not be laid at George Best's door. Because the disenchantment seemed to be almost throughout the team. A losing spell saps players' confidence and it is an enormous job to revive them. But the summer break came mercifully and that meant a rest from the tensions and worries and the hope that, with a brand new season ahead of them, the recent past might well be forgotten, especially since the players were well aware that they had been five points ahead in the first half of the season and could not suddenly have lost the ability that run had shown them to have.

It was not to be. The depression was still there. It was not just the losing of matches. It was the manner of losing. The players seemed to be devoid of fight and spirit. Frank O'Farrell bought Wyn Davies from Manchester City and Ted MacDougall from Bournemouth, but better results were still not forthcoming.

Around this time George Best had evidently not turned up for training. Players were fined now and again by Frank O'Farrell but on this particular occasion he said he would like the board to discuss the problem of George Best. The feeling of the board, expressed in Mr O'Farrell's presence, was that it would be a good idea if George Best was brought to a meeting with the board to get his own version of the whole matter. In the end it was decided by the directors that Louis Edwards and I should see Best.

Frank O'Farrell agreed to this and indeed, at the meeting wherein it was decided, tried to contact Best, but he was unsuccessful. The next day Louis Edwards went over to the United training headquarters at The Cliff, saw Frank O'Farrell and asked would he try to contact Best. Mr O'Farrell asked Pat Crerand to try to find Best and Pat failed to do so.

Again the next day Louis Edwards phoned the club, spoke to Frank O'Farrell, and asked for Pat Crerand, who, once again, went off looking for Best. This time he found him and took him to Louis Edwards's office at his business premises. After a short chat the chairman decided to join me with Best, as had been decided, with Mr O'Farrell's agreement, at that meeting two nights earlier. I was speaking at a Rotary lunch at Cheadle. The chairman phoned me there at 3.15 and I joined up with Louis Edwards and George Best at around 4 p.m.

The matter was discussed with Best and he was told that if he began training his position would be reviewed at the next board meeting. In turn Mr Edwards said that we must phone the other directors and Frank O'Farrell. The chairman phoned Mr O'Farrell and was told he was out. Ten minutes later Frank O'Farrell phoned Louis Edwards and the chairman told him we had seen Best and that Best was intending to start training and that the matter would be discussed at the next board meeting.

When Louis Edwards spoke to Frank O'Farrell again, the chairman said that there should be a statement to the Press, or a Press conference, because the public might have been given the impression that the board had been doing things behind his back. Mr O'Farrell said he did not think this a good thing as he had other things to do. Mr Edwards decided to make a statement to the Press.

I was contacted by one of George Best's business associates, who said that George would like to come and see me. *I said I could not see him as this would be dishonourable to the manager, Frank O'Farrell, and to the board.* If that was not non-interference I would like to know what is.

The following day Best went off to London, and I know that he was upset that I turned down his request to see me.

Considering that there had not been any interference of any description with Frank O'Farrell's management, it was all the more depressing to read criticism of the board by a local sports-writer and a follow-up story in a Sunday newspaper that Frank O'Farrell had thanked the local sports-writer for his article. He showed the board a letter he had written to the Sunday newspaper man saying that the article had embarrassed him, and the reply, but the public were not told this by Mr O'Farrell.

The Second Division was staring us in the face. The team had lost all fight. There were observations by a number of senior players that there did not seem to be a close enough relationship between manager and players. I have always felt strongly about the importance of close personal contact between managers, coaches and players. When I was a young player with Manchester City's third team, Albert Alexander was in charge there and he used to say to me: 'You will have to get sharp away.' I was probably not used to the English pace and it was good advice, pointing out a deficiency I had not seen in myself, but they were the only words ever spoken to me as a player that could remotely be termed coaching. In those days team sheets were the only arbiters of your form – first team, second team or third team. Nobody realized that a young player needed reassurance, but I certainly needed it. I had an inferiority complex and felt out of my depth.

Looking back I should be grateful for the gap that existed between manager and player then, and even between first-team players and also-rans, because it made me see that communication, respect and affection were essential – just as essential as expert knowledge of the theory of the game – to give players confidence and made them work well together as a team.

Of Frank O'Farrell Denis Law later said: 'He came a stranger and went a stranger.'

Frank O'Farrell was brought to the club to manage players. It seemed as if he wanted to manage the board, too. But the fact is this: *All the time he was at Old Trafford Frank O'Farrell never had anything but wholehearted support from his directors.*

I personally never went near the training quarters during the whole of Frank O'Farrell's managership. I never at any time had anything to do with teams and selections. In fact the directors did not know the team until just before the match. He never discussed players or teams except when he was on the point of buying, or wanted to buy, a player. My reply if he mentioned it to me was always: 'That is your business, Frank. In the end you will be held responsible and I will support you in getting the player.' And I always did.

I defy Frank O'Farrell to say that he had not the full support of his directors at all times.

Eventually, after the 5–0 defeat at Crystal Palace's ground, the board decided unanimously, having considered all these factors, that Frank O'Farrell must go. But they also decided that his contract would be honoured in full – and he was on probably the biggest salary of any manager in English football.

I will remind readers that at the beginning of this book having insisted on full control of players and playing matters, I acknowledged that if I were to fail the board were entitled to throw me out.

I repeat that people who put all the blame on George Best are being unjust.

My only self-criticism is that, with my experience, I *should* have interfered and, that I *should* have defended myself in answer to critics – in the game and out of it or in it once and now out – who had no knowledge of the position, some of whom should have known better because they would claim to know *me*. I don't mind criticism if it is just.

Frank O'Farrell was not at a loss for words at board meetings. In fact he most certainly is a talker. And he could always state a case very convincingly indeed. I do not recall any board meeting arguments with him about manager's reports, requests or suggestions. I do not remember any time that he asked me for advice. We talked on general terms about things generally, he and I, but ask me for advice? Never.

So we had hired and fired two managers. I do not say we were wrong when we made the choice. I do say we turned out to be wrong. But Wilf McGuinness seemed to be making a success in Greece. Frank O'Farrell may make a success elsewhere.

DOCTOR'S ORDERS

One of the liveliest characters in the Scotland team when I managed it was a little fellow called Tommy Docherty.

He was good to have around, a happy lad, full of patter, full of good humour, though the bite in his tackle would seem to deny it, as Celtic, Preston North End, Arsenal and (briefly) Chelsea supporters would affirm. He became coach at Chelsea and then manager, and produced a group of highly-talented young players who brought some success but never quite fulfilled themselves or Tommy.

Then followed Tommy's nomadic period, taking in the managerships of Rotherham United, Queen's Park Rangers (for about a month!) and Aston Villa, next appearing in Portugal, then in Hull, then becoming Scotland's team manager and then joining Manchester United.

His attitude was always as fiercely enthusiastic as his tackling. His patter increased in his early years of managership rather than diminished. In his early managerial days he seemed to me to be a little too keen to be *seen* to be a disciplinarian. But he *could* get performances out of players, which showed that they respected him.

He is a little older and much wiser now. I was always certain in my mind that he had plenty to offer football. I was equally certain that Scotland would benefit from his enthusiasm and judgement of players and their characters. Scotland needed cheering up when he arrived on the scene, and the change in atmosphere seemed to be immediate. The team's performances under his management showed that some of the old pride was coming back.

On the dismissal of Frank O'Farrell, the Manchester United directors decided to approach the Scottish Football Association, through Louis Edwards, to seek permission to approach Tommy Docherty. We hoped the new, more mature, but still effervescent, enthusiastic, still extrovert, warm, and never remote Docherty could bring happy days back to Old Trafford. Jimmy Aitken, president of the Scottish FA replied: 'I'll give you an answer within twenty-four hours after discussing it with my colleagues.' The Scots did give such permission, Tommy immediately said he would be delighted to come to Old Trafford, and he signed a contract.

I believe that notwithstanding his success with the Scottish team and the joy of *building* a team for his own country he had missed the English soccer scene, in which a manager is involved in matches constantly, every week and even twice a week sometimes, rather than every few months as international team managers are.

Why pick Tommy Docherty? I believe there are good reasons. He did remarkably well at Chelsea, a good building job. He still has admirers there, and more, too, at Aston Villa and Rotherham United. And he did bring new life to the Scotland team.

I personally knew of his happy disposition from his days under me for Scotland. I do not have to be told that a happy disposition alone will not win any medals. But Tommy combines humour and warmth and toughness. And happiness is one of the essentials. Tommy, like Bill Shankly, always seems to have a quip for the occasion, though he is as deadly earnest a man as any in football when earnestness is called for.

'Don't let Jim Holton near that place – it's a china shop,' was a typical Docherty touch. So was his crack after little Lou Macari's car accident: 'He only got away with it because he was thrown into the glove compartment.'

A laugh goes a long way when a team is struggling.

Tommy Docherty is so proud that any infringement on his dignity would arouse him to great anger. But he is not too proud to seek advice. Nor was I. I asked for advice from Jimmy Seed and Joe Edelston (father of Maurice) because I wanted to benefit from their vast experience, and benefit from it I did. There would be things Tommy could have advised me about and I would not have been too proud to seek his advice. Don Revie was not too proud to ask my advice.

When he first joined Manchester United Tommy Docherty said to me: 'I want you to promise if you see me doing anything drastically wrong or saying anything silly you will tell me.' More than once he said to me: 'Can we have five minutes' chat? I've been thinking . . .' and we would discuss his thoughts. 'What would you do?' he would ask. I would tell him and add: 'Tommy, whatever you decide after my advice you will be right in deciding what to do.'

Because football is a battle for existence. The manager is the commander. He uses all the brains of all the men in his command. And then he decides. He knew I wanted no part in picking his team for him. I had said it so often. I had had enough of all that. But Tommy said in public: 'How silly I would be not to ask advice of a man with Matt Busby's experience.'

Many managers asked me for advice. Don Revie was one. And Jimmy Armfield came to me and told me he had been offered the Bolton Wanderers managership. What would I advise? he asked, and I said: 'If you don't take it on you will never know. I would advise you to have a go.' And Jimmy went straight from me to Burnden Park and accepted the job.

The ghost of Herbert Chapman resides at Arsenal, with a bust of the great man, like a poltergeist, looking upon all who enter as if to remind them of the past glories.

It has been said many times by many critics publicly and privately that to give a successor a chance I should get out of Old Trafford. The implication is that a manager will constantly be looking over his shoulder to see if I am watching him, fearful lest what he does will not meet with my approval.

I hope that my declaration about my non-interference with team decisions, transfer decisions or any decisions concerning players during the Wilf McGuinness and Frank O'Farrell eras will help change the attitude of these critics.

What they are asking me to do is to tear my own heart out. How could I leave the place? How could I walk out of a club I built on the ashes of war and rebuilt after the mass tragedy of Munich, a club I love dearly, a club I have nearly killed myself for? And would it not be a wicked waste, I ask in all humility, to go home and shut myself in and muse on all the experience I have gained and let it rot there with me?

Tommy Docherty soon let it be known that he was not too proud to have me about the place and they don't come prouder than Tommy.

I do not know how successful he will be. I don't know how much or how little my advice will be sought by him. And if he seeks it I do not know how much or little it will help him. But surely even my critics must believe I would not do anything to hinder him or anyone else in his stewardship of the club for which I have shed blood. I am now a Manchester United director. I know more than the average director. I know too much to make a fool of myself by doing the very things I would not have put up with when I was manager.

The bust of Herbert Chapman is not there to haunt or to frighten people. I believe it is not only a symbol of past glories. I believe it is an inspiration for others to reach the same heights and higher, at once as an example of a challenge.

In my case the answer to my presence at Old Trafford, doing the volume of work that still comes my way, is with the manager himself. His own personality will emerge. It would be a self-eclipse if it didn't, or perhaps he would be the wrong horse for this particular course.

But with the success that will surely come to Manchester United again he will deserve the plaudits, his personality will shine through like the rays of the sun, and he will rightly be able to say: 'So much for the ghost of Matt Busby.'

And I will be the happiest man in football for him.

MY LEGACY

Loud critics found excuse in Manchester United's desperately poor 1972-3 season to suggest that the legacy of players I left to Wilf McGuinness and Frank O'Farrell left much to be desired.

Mr Brian Clough, that eminent solver of other teams' problems, went so far as to say in sympathizing with Mr O'Farrell: 'If, when Matt was manager, United had bought Roy McFarland (£24,000), John O'Hare (£21,000), John McGovern (£7,000), Alan Hinton (£29,000) and Kevin Hector (£40,000) – all of whom played in the Derby championship winning side – perhaps all those big fees Frank O'Farrell has had to pay would not have been necessary.' What nonsense.

My own view is that many managers would not have minded having the legacy I left. Let us examine it. First, I must say I have always considered that a player's best years are between twenty-six and thirty-two. There are limitless examples to prove it. Some go on longer and make tremendous contributions, like Jack Charlton, Bobby Charlton, Tony Book, and many others.

None of the players I handed over was thirty-two. Bobby Charlton and Bill Foulkes were about thirty-one with years of football left in them – Bobby, of course, was in the next year's World Cup in 1970. Pat Crerand and Denis Law were about twenty-eight and nowhere near the end of their playing days. Denis played for Scotland in 1971-2 season. Nobby Stiles had plenty left to offer. Alec Stepney, our goalkeeper, David Sadler and the boy Brian Kidd won England caps. Tony Dunne was a regular Eire international. Young John Aston had played the game of his life against Benfica in the

European Cup Final. Francis Burns was a Scotland Under-23 international, and George Best, one of the greatest footballers in the world, looked good for another ten years.

From Burnley I bought Willie Morgan, who became a key man for Scotland, and years could be expected from him. And I left the best part of £1 million to fill any gaps according to the judgement of my successor.

Why didn't I buy a centre-half for when Bill Foulkes was done? That is the question asked most critically. My answer is that I had tried to sign suitable centre-halves, but failed to get the ones I wanted. And I had felt for some time that a young one of our own, Steve James, would make a player of the right standard. Steve disappointed for a while, but late in the 1972-3 season he began to fulfil his own potential and, I hope, justify my judgement.

These players took Wilf McGuinness to three semi-finals. In Frank O'Farrell's first season Manchester United led the First Division by five points in December.

If they later became a poor legacy it must have been an extraordinary deterioration.

But I also left a long tradition of faithful supporters, and the power to attract large crowds in home or away matches or indeed anywhere on earth we visited. Judged by the many times in a season the ground we visited had to be closed, full to the brim, with thousands locked out, even in our unhappy 1972-3 season, I imagine we were fairly popular with other members of the First Division on that count alone.

Why did Manchester United consistently attract huge attendances, home and away? Why had we done so for a quarter of a century? Other clubs were known to express surprise, after achieving some success, even considerable success over a few years, that they were unable to match our attendances. 'What do our supporters want?' they cried. I do not know what their supporters wanted except that whatever Manchester United had the other teams' supporters seem to like it.

So I must set down what I believe were the reasons for our pulling power.

First, we had consistent success, not only for five, six or even ten years, but for well over twenty years. But that is not all.

Second, consistently through that quarter-century, in

Above. An overhead kick from Matt to clear his goal – in his early days as a Manchester City defender.

Below. The 'Busby babes' – the United team just before Munich: *left to right, standing:* Tom Curry (trainer)*, Duncan Edwards*, Mark Jones*, Ray Wood, Bobby Charlton, Bill Foulkes, Matt Busby; *seated:* John Berry, Bill Whelan*, Roger Byrne*, David Pegg*, Eddie Colman*. The starred players died and so did Tommy Taylor and Geoff Bent who are not in this group.

The bodies of the Munich victims.

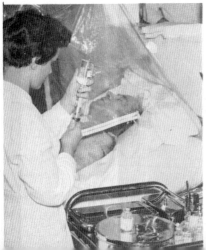

Matt Busby 'doing badly' in an oxygen tent in his Munich hospital.

'King' Law wins the high ball.

One of soccer's legendary figures – the great
Tom Finney taking a water slide.

Wonder-goalkeeper Trautmann making a save.

A United 'boy' cleaning the boots. It is the young George Best, seated, centre.

Real master, di Stefano, one of the great international figures.

Bobby (in the dark vest) versus Jack. He didn't get the goal this time.

George Best again, caught by his shirt by Fulham's Fred Callaghan.

The climax of Matt Busby's and United's career, the European Cup (1968). *Left to right, top*: Foulkes, Aston, Rimmer, Stepney, Gowling, Herd; *middle*: Sadler, Dunne, Brennan, Crerand, Best, Burns, trainer Jack Crompton; *front*: Ryan, Stiles, Law, Busby, Charlton, Kidd, Fitzpatrick.

Mercer, Alexander and Allison.

Matt Busby and Frank O'Farrell watch United's defeat by Fulham, 2-1.

Tommy Docherty on top of his form.

The 'new' boss, Wilf McGuiness talks to United players while Sir Matt (far right) looks on, smiling.

Knight Commander of St. Gregory. 1972. Jean applies the finishing touches.

achieving our successes or even when we had the odd mediocre seasons as far as actual trophies were concerned, we provided the spectators with something worth watching for itself, win, lose, or draw. We provided attractive, exciting, positive football of a standard that, once seen, people wanted to see again. But my first two reasons alone are not the complete answer.

It would be unreasonable if I did not pay tribute to the tremendous number of people who rallied to Manchester United's cause after the Munich disaster. People came to Old Trafford who had not been there before. Their desire was to help, to show that behind us in our efforts to live again were the hearts of people who had never even seen football. I do not feel I am being over-dramatic if I compare the rallying call of people determined not to let us go under with the rallying call of people whose way of life is threatened by an enemy at war. People cried in the streets, I have been told so by many who saw them. They flocked to our aid. They willed us through. They came and they stayed.

But this also is only another contributory cause of Manchester United's drawing power. Because this rallying to our cause could not, of itself, have lasted. Generations change. And as a new generation emerges, wars become mere stories by fathers and grandfathers, and the young ones live for *now*, though, by habit, a greater number of them became 'United' because they were 'weaned' that way by relations who had rallied to aid us. In any case we had, from 1945, *always* been blessed with tremendous support. So, for the old faithfuls and the new loyalists we had to provide, in return for their faith and loyalty, yet another new team for them and us to be proud of and to enjoy, and to argue and boast about, and for them to moan at us about if we had the cheek not to win at least two prizes a season.

I believe the fourth of my reasons completes the picture and gives an answer to those who ask about magic magnetism. Here it is:

 Manchester United always had, throughout that quarter-century, great entertainers, great individuals, great stars, players who fitted into the pattern I was always trying to perfect yet who could produce something from nothing, or who made people gasp or laugh with the sheer enjoyment of seeing something different, something surprising, something creative, something extraordinary, something extemporaneous, something exciting for its sheer impudence or audacity, something graceful, explosive, beautiful.

Great players? Take a few of them – Johnny Carey, Jack Rowley, the incomparable Duncan Edwards, Tommy Taylor, Denis Law, Bobby Charlton, George Best. I need hardly go on.

How the old Hollywood star-makers would have blurbed a film starring filmland's equivalent of Charlton, Law and Best is interesting to cogitate on. And taking the case of films to its conclusion, I would say that people will flock to see Elizabeth Taylor, or Peter O'Toole or some such, in a good, bad or mediocre film because these players have that magical something that makes them stars. Manchester United always had stars.

Those, then, are my four reasons, four causes that brought us such splendid effects. And I would sum up like this:

As far as entertainment is concerned, some critics and managers are apt to go overboard about showmanship for itself alone, confusing it with entertainment. Certainly entertainment and attractive football should not be confused with playing what is termed the 'professional' way, with boring possession play, showing off when you are three or four goals up, over-indulging in the clever stuff, which is not all that clever, and taking the tip-tapping mickey out of a team already well beaten, which is as embarrassing to the spectator as to the victims. No, that sort of stuff will not bring the people in or keep those already in .

The right idea is to make your game entertaining from the *start*, or try to, home or away, by making it *positive*, uninhibited by fear. And then, if you have any real stars, add a bit of stardust to taste. And keep it all up for twenty years.

That's all.

MY MEMORIAL

Some admirers asked me if they could commission a bust for me to go on permanent display at Old Trafford. I said no. Others wanted to organize a testimonial for me. I said no.

Because my memorial is the three great teams I created

for Manchester United in twenty-three years of manager-ship.

But which of the three do I rate the best? Old-timers may say the 1948 FA Cup-winning side, my first one. Younger ones, and some old-timers, will say the pre-Munich team, the Babes. And there are those who, because of the magic of Charlton, Law and Best, will say the European Cup-winning team of 1968, albeit without the injured Law.

They were all great teams, but I have no doubt in my mind at all. The pre-Munich team was potentially the best club side I have seen, about to take over that crown from Real Madrid when the Munich crash ended them. They won the First Division Championship twice, the first time by eleven points, reaching the European Cup semi-final twice, and the FA Cup Final once, all while still in their infancy.

But all three *were* great teams nevertheless, and in their blending, building, and controlling posed different prob-lems of managership.

The 1948 team were mature when I came on the scene. Their varying personalities I have described. I was ten years older than their average age of twenty-five, but young enough to get among them, play with them, and stay among them. My job was to persuade them that we were all in football for the same purpose – to win. We could do so if we gave for each other until it hurt. They soon knew I knew what the game was all about, tactics and the rest, and I soon let them know that I wanted them to express themselves individually as well as demanding that they gave the lot to each other when help was needed. The respect we needed from each other was soon forthcoming. There were only rare rifts. And the affection which is my third essential rule for good managership followed. Their natural ability did the rest. There can have been few if any better club sides in the world in 1948.

The Babes were virtually my own from the cradle, ex-cepting the goalkeepers Ray Wood and later Harry Gregg, the right-winger Johnny Berry, and the centre-forward Tommy Taylor, our only imports from other clubs.

The age gap was much greater for me. I was more the father figure, less the elder brother I had been with the '48 team, though I could still get among them in training. Re-spect from younger ones is easier to come by, especially since great care was taken in housing them in good 'digs', and since men like Jimmy Murphy and Bert Whalley commanded respect quite instinctively. But unquestionably those boys would put a damaged leg into a tackle for me, and for each other. It was a family affection that went throughout the Old Trafford ground.

The United team won the Football Association Youth Cup every year from 1953 to 1957, so the pattern was there and scarcely needed working on. The big, strong Bill Foulkes and the speedy, high-class Roger Byrne, quite the best post-war left full-back were entirely complementary, as were the huge Duncan Edwards and the tiddler Eddie Colman, big Dunc monopolizing the entire proceedings, up scoring goals, back defending, little Eddie shimmying through the slenderest gaps in the opposition and foreseeing situations as if he were clairvoyant, creating openings for colleagues and havoc in the opposition.

We had splendid alternatives at centre-half, as different as centre-halves could be, but priceless inasmuch as we always had a top-class man in this vital spot. Jackie Blanchflower, brother of Danny, of course, was equally keen on playing artistic, creative, productive, positive football. He tackled well because like all top-class players he was a good reader of situations, but he scorned the big boot. Mark Jones was a big, strong defender in the Foulkes mould, a comforting figure to have behind you when you are under pressure.

So with creative players like Byrne, Edwards, Colman and Blanchflower and the others in a lesser way, producing telling passes from the back, our forwards were always well provided for. And a fearful quintet those forwards were to any opposition. It is hard to conceive what heights Billy Whelan would have reached. His control of the ball was immaculate. He beat opponents with consummate ease, put accurate passes around and shot neatly and tellingly. The other inside man, the local Dennis Viollet, also with adhesive ball-control in close situations, darted around creating panic among opposition defences and was a lethal finisher, as his thirty-two goals in the 1959-60 season later testified.

In between them was the tall, black-curly-haired Tommy Taylor, an Adonis even among footballers, the perfect spearhead whether the ball was in the air or on the ground. His heading was as hard as some players' shooting, his shooting with either foot, well controlled. He had a massive heart, a permanent smile, and yet was as shy as a footballer could possibly be. He never knew how good he was, and it came as a big surprise to him when soon after he joined United he was picked to play the first of his nineteen games for England.

At outside-right we had the small but devastating Johnny Berry, elusive, explosive, taking on man after man, nimbly and at tremendous speed, and as likely as not finishing off with a mighty shot the like of which made you wonder how so much power could be generated in so small a frame. He tore defences apart by sheer skill and speed. I knew this only too well when I signed him from Birmingham in 1951 for £25,000. He had scored one of his specials against us.

On the left wing, the neat, classy David Pegg was adept at getting out of tight situations by his own skill or by using other players perfectly. Then he would 'go' and then he would provide, because Pegg was a goal-maker rather than goal-taker. Albert Scanlon, very sharp, with a good shot, was a more direct player.

Bobby Charlton had just moved into the team by the time of the crash, and we had also more home-grown talents like Freddie Goodwin, Alex Dawson, Nobby Lawton, Nobby Stiles and Johnny Giles coming along.

There would have been nothing to touch this team for ten years. How good it would have become with experience it is impossible to imagine.

It took about five years to build the next team, and again building it and blending it needed different facets of managership from the first two. I had bought more players and more expensive players on the way back after Munich, like Albert Quixall (£45,000), Maurice Setters (£30,000), Noel Cantwell (£29,500), David Herd (£40,000), Denis Law (£115,000), Pat Crerand (£43,000), Graham Moore (£35,000), John Connelly (£56,250) and Alec Stepney (£52,000). Of these, David Herd had a particularly good partnership with Denis Law, big David's power and strength taking much weight off Denis, who also found him a perfect foil for his old one-two wall pass, since David wasn't one to nurse the ball and Denis liked the quick one back because then his sharp reflexes were exploited to the full. So both scored plenty of goals.

There was no pattern to begin with, but it was still a happy club, usually knocking around one prize or another. The players gave me all they had. The respect was mutual and immediate, affection soon followed no matter whether the players were imported or home-grown. Few Manchester United players asked for transfers in my time. I could not get among these players in actual practice combat as I had the other two teams, but I was never far from them.

But it was practically my own family of sons who actually won the European Cup at Wembley, because, since Denis Law was injured and out of the Final, no fewer than nine of the eleven were virtually brought up at Old Trafford, including David Sadler and Tony Dunne who cost me next to nothing. The heights they reached in that Final showed what affection can bring to a team. Their efforts in extra time were superhuman.

Perhaps the player who did most in achieving the blend and the old pattern was Pat Crerand. Pat was a courageous player. Adept with the long pass, he would nevertheless send a rare one astray. This did not deter him. His next pass would be as long. And, as young players would confirm, Pat was always there, though he had some comical confessions to make about not being a speed merchant, when they most needed help. I believe Crerand was irreplaceable. I would have played him a bit longer than he was played.

When people with hindsight tell me what mistakes I have made I reply: 'I am never wrong. I may later turn out not to have been right but my decision was not wrong when I made it.'

My biggest regret is that I did not sign Jack Charlton for £26,000 before Don Revie's time at Leeds. But Munich had crippled United financially and I decided I could not afford it. I converted Bill Foulkes to centre-half instead, but I often wonder how much stronger we would have been with Foulkes at No 2 and big Jack at No 5.

Years later I wanted a player who was available for transfer. Another manager rang me, because, he said, we didn't want to indulge in an auction. He and I agreed a fee we would offer, so that it would be up to the player and his club to choose between us. Next I heard was that the manager who had rung me had signed the player for £10,000 more than he and I had agreed on. I don't call that a mistake, unless keeping your word is a mistake.

OFF THE FIELD

If the manager asks for advice the directors are there to give it, even if, as it will be remembered old Harold Hardman said about me: 'The manager has asked for advice and we'll give it to him and then he'll please his bloody self.' More particularly the chairman and the board are there to back the man they themselves have backed as a likely winner. I am a firm believer still in my old philosophy that if the position at the top is not right it will not be right anywhere, and I do not care where it applies, if that backing is not wholehearted and unanimous, or if there are opposing factions on a board, no matter what success is achieved in the short term, lasting success will not follow.

At Manchester United it was right at the top because my three chairmen, the first two after some preliminary skirmishing with me as I have said, have made it so. There was no skirmishing between Louis Edwards and me at all. For months before the Munich disaster the late chairman, Harold Hardman, and his directors had been looking for another man to add strength to the board. Luckily for all of us Louis Edwards turned out to be the man.

Louis Edwards could not have been brought on to the United board at a more difficult time. We needed all the strength we could muster. He became a director just after the crash. One of the directors said to him then: 'We have no team now. Do you still want to come on to the board?' and he said: 'Of course I do.' He was one of Manchester United's great signings. I had known this man for many years. I knew his qualities. I knew his fibre. I knew he was right for Manchester United. Our record since he arrived on the board in 1958 will stand anybody's examination.

In June 1965 our chairman, Harold Hardman, died, aged eighty-three, after fifty loving years on the board, a half-century of service which followed a career that included playing for Everton, Blackpool and for England.

Louis Edwards was made chairman. Together we have

travelled to practically every part of the world where football is played. He has given much of his business time (luckily for the business, his brother Douglas, is not a football fanatic like Louis), and he has given much of his domestic time (luckily his wife, Muriel, likes watching United) in the club's cause. He has given his business experience and his energy and enthusiasm to the club. He has given it extra stability. He does not ask a person to do a job and then try to do it himself. He does not ask anybody to do a job without giving him his full backing, and I cannot remember having an argument with him. If I had an idea about something he would push me towards it. If I said I wanted such and such a player he would say: 'Go and get him.'

We differ in one regard, and it has brought me nearly to apoplectic fits in places all over the globe.

Louis Edwards is a naturally happy man. Nothing ever seems to get him down. He is happy even first thing in the morning, when I have to confess I am not at my sparkling best, especially after some occasion that has required a glass or two or more of champagne or Scotch. Absolutely the opposite is Louis Edwards. There I would be, mooning around my hotel room wearing my sombre look and not wishing to exchange the time of day with anybody just yet, thank you very much. Then a cheerful whistle would approach from without, followed by the jarring sound of a knock on the door, and in would walk Louis Edwards himself, as large as life, full of the joy of living, and planning the cheerful day ahead.

Such spirit in such a man is nevertheless catching at less difficult times of the day, and permeates, especially in a place like a football ground, where good cheer can improve the output and even win matches. I don't know how he maintains this cheerfulness so constantly and so consistently. But it is as well he does. The problems of football are enough in a happy club.

The vice-chairman of the United board is Alan Gibson, son of the late, great United benefactor. Bill Young, Denzil Haroun JP, and Martin Edwards, son of the chairman, are the other directors, all quiet men who, like Louis Edwards, seek neither publicity nor anything else but the good of Manchester United. And, I almost forgot, there is another, the junior director – Matt Busby.

The loss of our secretary, Walter Crickmer, in the crash, was like losing the irreplaceable. He had so many things at his finger-tips or in his memory box that it seemed impossible for anybody else to know so much. This is a big job in any football club but at Manchester United, which by 1958 seemed to be in touch with most parts of the world as well as with the large domestic population of the Football League, it was a huge one. So many things depend upon our secretary, the least of which could cause calamity if left undone or if not done properly. Items like travel, hotels, fixture re-arrangements, attendance problems, tickets, contracts, minutes and literally hundreds of other necessities must come within the orbit of the secretary.

We had a young fellow as assistant secretary, a quietish diligent character called Leslie Olive. He was himself so good a goal-keeper that I called on him at least twice to help me out of trouble by playing in the first team. Luckily for us he was an even better administrator. But he was not always appreciated to the full, he felt, and, like a sort of Oliver Twist, he once asked for more – pay that is. The board were not all that keen on obliging the young assistant secretary. I think he was on the point of going abroad for fame and fortune. I persuaded the board that the young man was worth his pay-rise. 'He's an important cog in our wheel,' I said. He got it. And I seem to recall his wife, Betty, telling me much later that had it not been for me they would have been in some foreign land.

As it was he turned out to be another of our home-grown babes who grew to sturdy manhood, in a job that grows ever bigger, even more onerous. Nobody who did not know Leslie Olive very well would call him laughing boy. In fact he has a lively sense of humour. But with the number of problems he has continually to solve he simply hasn't the time to be everybody's meat for a long chat. Manchester United have more regular supporters than any team in Britain, if not the world. There must be 50,000 of them anyway. But when tickets for the biggest games are printed the number jumps to about 200,000 who say they watch us home and away and have done for thirty years.

A man with just that single problem – though he has a staff to deal with tickets it is still his problem – doesn't need any more. And Les has plenty more.

Les Olive does a fine job. He is well on top of it. He is another who finds it unnecessary to make loud noises.

SIR MATT

My CBE (1958) and knighthood (1968) were for services to football. It could be that these services included running the Army team in aid of various causes, one of which brought me a letter from Mrs Churchill, which I cherish. At around the same time as I received this letter, I remember Lord Montgomery, fresh from his Middle East campaign, coming to an England-Scotland match. As captain of the Scots I had a brief chat with him before presenting the Scottish players to him. 'I have a confession to make,' he said to me. 'I have never been to Scotland.'

Now the difference between a field-marshal and a sergeant-major is so vast as to be comprehended only by a soldier, so what possessed me to be brave or bold enough to make a wisecrack to the mighty man I shall never know. 'You ought to be ashamed of yourself, sir,' I said. But instead of sticking me on a fizzer (Army form B 252, whilst on active service etc., etc., better known as a charge or a fizzer), Monty merely smiled the enigmatic smile that matched the Mona Lisa's and haunted Rommel.

The next Scotland-England match, at Hampden Park, Glasgow, was to be favoured by a visit by King George VI, but illness prevented this and Monty duly arrived to do the honours. First words he said to me as I was about to introduce the Scottish players to him were: 'You see I'm here, sergeant-major.'

It is not only an *honour* to receive honours. It is a privilege. They carry with them the attendant opportunities for enjoyable and educational experiences. Tea with the Queen and Prince Philip and their family is an entertaining occasion. They are all very easy to talk to, and Prince Charles soon showed that he knows what is going on in the football world when he asked me: 'Any managers been sacked this morning?'

Perhaps the honour that touched me most was being made a Freeman of Manchester in 1967, only the sixty-sixth, and the first of the sporting fraternity. After all, I am a Scot, notwithstanding forty-odd years in Manchester, and it came as a wonderful surprise to me that my affection for my adopted City which Jean and I have for long loved dearly, was so magnificently reciprocated. If this sounds sentimental, all right, then I am sentimental. If I have done some little thing for Manchester it is scant repayment for the things Manchester has done for me.

Because Manchester is people, Manchester United is people, and the Stretford End is people, and Salford is people. If there are warmer people than these, I in my travels many times round the world have not met them. And I speak not merely as a football manager who was blessed with some success but as a young Scot coming to a strange place, away from home for the first time in his life, and a struggling footballer who had plenty of heartbreak before he reached the top. Only with a wife like mine and friends like ours could this story have been told.

PART TWO

FOUR TO REMEMBER

DUNCAN EDWARDS

At fifteen, the boy from Dudley, Worcestershire, who came to Manchester United was a man already. He looked like a man. He played like a man.

He was born on 1 October 1936. On 4 April 1953, aged sixteen, he made his League debut. In 1954 he played in England's first Under-23 International team, and at the age of eighteen years and 183 days he became the youngest player to play for England.

Duncan Edwards was then, and has always remained to me, incomparable. His death after the Munich crash in 1958 when he was only twenty-one, but with eighteen caps already, was as far as football is concerned the biggest single tragedy that has happened to England and to Manchester United. I believe he would have been playing for England still. He seemed indestructible.

He was a Colossus first among the boys and then among the men. In his early days Jimmy Murphy and I would go to watch him with the juniors and try to find some fault with him. He seemed too good to be true. We could find nothing wrong with the lad. What could we work on? Nothing. Whatever was needed he had it. He was immensely powerful. He was prodigiously gifted in the arts and crafts of the game. His temperament was perfect.

Work-rate, which became fashionable much later, would never even have had to be mentioned to Duncan. He couldn't have enough matches. And he couldn't find enough work in any of them. He was utterly indefatigable.

His confidence from being a boy was supreme and infectious. As we were going away he would say to all around him, the great and the greater (our players at that time were all great): 'Well, lads, we haven't come here for nuffin.' And he saw to it that we seldom came away with nuffin. If things were not going well up front or we needed a goal we would say: 'Shove Duncan up.' And Duncan would shove himself up and bang one or two goals in. He must have been an absolute nightmare for opposition goalkeepers, for this lad who could belt over a pass from one side of the pitch to the other with the most amazing accuracy and power was equally powerful and accurate when he blazed in a shot from any distance up to forty yards. Just the sight of Duncan blasting his way up the pitch with the ball was enough to scare the bravest goalkeeper to death.

In a match in West Germany, Duncan picked up a ball in midfield, feinted as if to pass it, bypassed a couple of opponents and suddenly hit the ball from about twenty-five to thirty yards out and with such power that it was in the net before anybody realized it. Not surprisingly after that the Germans named him 'Boom Boom'.

No opponent was too big or too famous for Duncan. When he went into the tackle he seldom came away without the ball. He was as fair as he was powerful. But opponents would bounce off him. He was as good with the delicacies of the short pass as with the space-consuming long pass.

I remember saying to him once: 'Keep an eye on Ronnie (Cope). He might need a lift.' Duncan kept an eye on Ronnie and did about half a dozen other jobs besides. A wing-half, he could have been a great centre-half or a great forward striker. He would have been one of the great leaders with his sheer inspiration. He inspired by his sheer presence, by his sheer enthusiasm. If there was ever a player who could be called a one-man team that man was Duncan Edwards.

He was the most valuable member of one team I ever saw anywhere. He was worth two of most and two good ones at that. We seldom lost a match, but if we did, most players, as most players will, tried to banish defeat from their minds. Not Duncan. It didn't finish there. He regarded defeat as a personal reflection on himself. 'What am I doing letting that lot beat us?' he would say.

He was full of life, full of football. He used to come and ask me could he play in the youth team. He would play every day in the week if he could. I know players, like the rest of us, can have too much football, but when I hear some of the complaints by some of them about too many games I always think of Duncan Edwards. He would have thought they must be mad. He played more than ninety games in one extended season for United and England teams. And no player did more per match than Duncan.

He was never in an ounce of trouble. He never went out gallivanting at night. The pictures were about his only night-life. He lived for the game and was concerned only with making himself and keeping himself fit for it.

Goodness only knows what impact Duncan Edwards would have made on the game had he been spared. Any manager asked what he would like for Christmas would have said: 'I would like a Duncan Edwards, please.'

Duncan suffered terrible injuries in the crash. In some of my rare moments of consciousness I heard the sounds of suffering. It was Duncan. Then one day, in another moment of awareness, I heard a clergyman in the hospital say: 'Duncan is dead.' The clergyman was given a telling off for saying such a thing anywhere near me, but that was when I first began to be really aware that something awful had happened. I was afraid to ask but I asked.

Duncan Edwards the fighter fought his vain fight for more than two weeks.

Yes, I feel quite certain that the youngest England player would have grown to be the eldest.

BOBBY CHARLTON

From an old oak called Tanner Milburn sprang many mighty acorns, some called Milburn and some called Charlton. Old Tanner's genes had at least one thing in common. When they kicked they kicked like a mule. There was George, Jack, Jim and Stan Milburn, among them full-backs who were good chaps to move out of the way of when they were taking free kicks. If you didn't you would go down like a skittle. Some people are born with hard shots. None can be taught how to have a hard shot. If a lad can't kick the ball hard when he is six he will not kick it hard when he is sixteen or twenty-six or thirty-six, and I don't care who tries to teach him. If he is going to kick it hard he will kick it hard at six, sixteen, and twenty-six, and even sixty-six. It has nothing to do with how big he is. Either he can or he can't. It is one of the mysteries. It is called timing.

So those full-backs could kick that ball with immense power, but also cleanly, crisply. There was another Milburn who also whacked the ball hard. But he was a forward. He was Jackie. He played for Newcastle United.

He became beloved by Geordies throughout the land as Wor Jackie. He had the happy knack of gathering the ball quickly, looking at the goal, and, wham! – the goalkeeper next saw the ball at the back of the net.

The Milburns and the Charltons were all good footballers, all hard shots, and all nice fellows to boot.

In 1953 a small, fair-haired Geordie boy of fifteen, from old Tanner's Ashington, name of Bobby Charlton, arrived at Old Trafford. He was grandson of Tanner, nephew of George, Jack, Jim and Stan Milburn, second cousin of Wor Jackie Milburn and brother of Jack, of Leeds United, who was later to play in Sir Alf Ramsey's 1966 World Cup-winning England team with Bobby. It was soon shown that the boy, who was as shy as they come (and at fifteen, miles away from home, they come very shy as a rule) and quiet by any standards, had inherited old Tanner's gift for hitting the ball with a great thump and for great distances. That was only one of his many qualities – so many, indeed, that they combined to form a genius. It was quickly evident that Master Bobby was going to make a considerable impact on football and on Manchester United football in particular.

Bobby played his first game against Charlton Athletic on 6 October 1956. Roger Byrne, Duncan Edwards and Tommy Taylor were playing for England that day (incidentally our Jackie Blanchflower was playing for Ireland against England). And Bobby had a sore ankle at that. But a small item like a painful ankle would never stop Bobby from playing a game of football. In fact he also showed that in the cause of Manchester United and England he would play anywhere.

He began his debut as if he was in his bare feet kicking a hot potato. He 'got rid' too quickly, very hard but too quickly. That must have been the only spell in which Bobby Charlton was ever nervous on a football pitch.

The nerves did not last many minutes. Suddenly he began to play his own game, and his own game was slipping gracefully past two opponents as if they were stakes in the ground and putting in a good pass or whacking in a terrific shot.

Thus he went past two opponents and shot a beauty, a goal from the moment he hit the ball. And he scored again and United won 4–2.

The saddest days for a manager are when he has to tell a young player he has not quite made the grade. The greatest thrill for a manager who has persuaded a boy to leave home and his parents to allow it is when the young seed bursts through and then blooms gloriously. None has bloomed more gloriously than Bobby Charlton. That big shot of his has thrilled the world. But nobody was more thrilled than I was that day, though I had already known he had that shot in his boots.

Never did a boy seem to enjoy his game more than Bobby did. If he had a fault it was that his long game was so good he overdid it. It is not much of a fault, and most professional footballers would like to have it. Bobby could put a pass with great accuracy across the full width of a pitch, a feat that needs to be tried to be appreciated. Few players can do it. It would take some of the greatest players two kicks to get the ball across the pitch. Bobby could do it in one as a mere boy.

The same with corner kicks. With scarcely any backlift Bobby could put a corner kick over the far post – either foot – with no effort at all. People who take corner kicks for granted should try this too. There are great professional footballers who could not put the ball over to the near post. As far as shooting at goal is concerned I cherish a memory of Bobby hitting a thigh-high centre into the net on the full volley in one of his earliest games.

But variety is invaluable in the big professional game, and I advised Bobby to mix it a bit, with a touch of the short stuff as well as the long. It did not take him long to mix it.

Bobby Charlton was just about clinching his regular place in Manchester United's senior team when the Munich disaster hit us. Miraculously thrown out of the stricken aircraft and virtually unhurt physically, though the shock must have been profound, this boy Charlton became a man overnight. From being one attractive new stone in a mighty edifice he became the foundation on which we had to rebuild over the ruins.

There was no more graceful sight on any soccer pitch in the world than Bobby Charlton going forward, seeming to glide past opponents. There is no man who dummied or changed direction better, no man better with the long pass or the short. There was no thrill greater than when he struck that ball for goal.

He was awarded the OBE. He has a World Cupwinning medal, a European Cupwinning medal, 106 England caps, League Championship and FA Cupwinning medals. He has scored more goals than any other man for England. Everything he could win he has won. He scarcely had time for a holiday for a decade, with his England and United commitments. He was idolized all over the earth from his twentieth year. There has never been a more popular footballer.

As a player, to suit the requirements of his club and country, he was a striking forward, a winger, or a deep-lying provider, always a creator of something from nothing, always a player of whom the unexpected was expected, who aroused gasps of anticipation every time he had the ball.

Out of all these stresses and strains, from the shy boy who had hardly a word for anyone emerged the mature football figure who, though he would shy from it by choice, and much to his own surprise, became adept at public speaking.

If there were any nervous breakdowns knocking around – and there seemed to be an epidemic of them in 1972 – Bobby was surely entitled to have one. But psychiatrists would be out of work if we were all like Bobby Charlton.

From all the adulation he was showered with, man and boy, for all his England caps and the rest, Bobby remained the same gentle heart he was as a boy, as near perfection as man and player as it is possible to be.

I have no doubt he nattered a bit on the pitch, but most likely to himself, and there was never anything vicious about him as player or man. There can be no better example to other footballers or to boys anywhere than Bobby Charlton.

But if he reads this I know perfectly well what he will say to me. He has said it before:

'You laid it on a bit thick, didn't you?'

A skinny wee boy with a squint fixed a paper ball to the clothes rack in his mother's kitchen in the home of an Aberdeen trawlerman. Then he pulled up the rack until he could not quite head that ball with his highest leap. Then, several leaps later, he could just touch it. Several leaps more and he could head it. Then he raised the rack until he could not quite reach it again. And so it went on until his mother told him she would be obliged if he would get from under her feet.

Not long later, the still skinny wee boy left home as we Scots are apt to do, in search of fame and the hope that a fortune might be thrown in. All he had in his favour were prodigious talents for football, an immense heart to go with them, but, by now, no squint. This elfin, tiddler facsimile of Tommy Steele, with fair thatch and big grin, was called Denis Law. He landed at Huddersfield Town, where the manager, Andy Beattie, not long afterwards turned down my magnanimous offer of £10,000 for young Denis, thus confirming what a cheek I had and what a good judge Andy was. The boy grew a bit and when still a mere boy made the Huddersfield first team. Every time I saw him the more I liked him, and when I accepted the managership of the Scotland team for a short time I pulled him in for his first international cap at eighteen. By then he was all of 5 ft. 9 in. and 10 st. He was an elf with a wallop.

Later he was transferred to Manchester City and not long after that was lured to Turin, where he quickly became so disenchanted with Italian football, as I have said, that eventually I bought him for £115,000, the most expensive signing I ever made. On achievement he turned out to be the cheapest.

But it may well be asked why I did not sign him from Huddersfield in the first place and therefore save more than £50,000 and have him for longer. The reason is that in the season 1959-60, near the end of which Law moved to Manchester City, our United team had scored 102 goals in finishing seventh so we did not seem in urgent need of a 'striker' (to use the with-it expression), especially since we had also by no means recovered financially from the Munich crash.

It was not until we had lost the 1961-2 FA Cup semi-final to Tottenham Hotspur by 3-1 that, having pondered during the game about what to do to add the essential finish to our good build-up moves, I decided that the man I would like above all others was Denis. I have described how we eventually signed him. Even the memory makes me feel travel-weary. But once he was with us I knew at first sight that we indeed had the most exciting player in the game. He was the quickest-thinking player I ever saw, seconds quicker than anyone else. He had the most tremendous accelera-tion. He leapt Olympian heights (remember the paper ball on his mother's clothes rack!).

He headed the ball with almost unbelievable accuracy and with the power of a shot. He had the courage to take on the biggest and most ferocious opponents. His passing was impeccable. He was one of the most unselfish players I have seen. If he was not in the best position to score he would give it to someone who was. But when a chance was on for him, or a half- or a quarter-chance, or a chance that was no sort of chance at all for anybody else but him, whether he had his back to goal, was sideways on, or the ball was on the deck or shoulder-height, he would have it in the net with such power and acrobatic agility that colleagues and opponents alike could only stand and gasp. No other player scored as many miracle goals as Denis Law. Goals that looked simple as Denis tapped them in were simple only because he got himself into positions so quickly that opponents just could not cope with him.

He was the first British player to salaam or salute the crowd. To start with it was the imp in him. Early on at Old Trafford the multitudes cheered him and the few who did not recognize his fun as fun perhaps jeered him, though not for long. Because he soon became what the crowd called him – 'The King'. And other scorers copied his salute, so that now the scorer of the flukiest goal of the season shoots an arm to the sky wherever football is played, on huge First Division grounds, on village greens, in streets where lamp-posts become goal-posts.

Denis was liable to do a cross-talk act with a referee or a linesman, complete with gesticulations. Some referees and some linesmen would reply in kind and make fun of it and suffer no loss of respect from Denis for it. Some were touchier, or perhaps they would call it tougher. Referees come in all sorts, the same as footballers and managers.

Denis Law, certainly, had more of his share of trouble with referees, more than his share of fines and suspensions. But it was the same very sharp reflexes, which made him the greatest man in the penalty box I ever saw, that also brought him into conflict with officialdom. Even in the ordinary scrimmaging for the ball Denis could be spotted a mile off. With his legs and arms flailing about in a bid to get the ball he looked twice as physically dangerous as he was. It was, indeed, very often the speed of his actions more than the actions themselves that brought him trouble, though I am not saying there were not times when he asked for all he got, no more so than when he chased Ian Ure (then with Arsenal but later Law's colleague at Old Trafford) all over the pitch to avenge himself for an excessively enthusiastic tackle. Off they both went for an early bath, these Scottish international team-mates.

After such occasions, but more often lightning-reflex actions of retaliation, I would say to Denis in the dressing room: 'When are you going to learn some sense? Getting sent off is bad for you and it is bad for the club. In fact it is good for nothing. You'll have to stop this nonsense.' And Denis would say: 'I know I'm in the wrong.' And I would say: 'Well for goodness sake count ten.' And Denis would say: 'I don't *want* to get in trouble. I don't *want* to embarrass the club, but it's no use me saying I won't do it again. If someone kicks me I can't promise I won't have a go at him.' Denis knew all about his quick reflexes. But his critics in this regard would not be so critical if they had seen his legs after many a game. I have seen them virtually slashed to ribbons, with blood and cuts all over the place. How much can any man stand? It isn't sporting to retaliate, it might be said. Sportsmen should be above that sort of thing. But body-contact sports cannot avoid a touch of spontaneous violence. Rugby Union has its share, and who would accuse Rugby Union players of not being sportsmen?

On only one occasion had I any trouble with Denis. A new contract was due to him, and he left me a note to say he was not satisfied and unless he got certain terms he would have to ask for a move. When I read the note I sent for him and said: 'If that's how you feel you can go.' But Denis was big enough to tell me he was only trying to push his luck, and big enough, too, to apologize. So Law and United were quickly reconciled and a good job it was for both.

There came a period when injury nagged at Denis. He suffered it stoically for a long time. There were people who thought he was laying it on a bit. I would ask how he felt, and he would answer: 'I'm all right until I have to move quickly. Then it's painful.' His phenominal speed thus curtailed, he couldn't be the old Law. And worst was that Denis himself was thrown into a fit of depression because he couldn't play to his own standards. But it was eventually discovered that a piece of cartilage had caused him absolute agony.

He overcame it all, and if he never quite reached his old heights, he still fought back to play for Scotland again, which is high enough for most people, and to show his friends of the Stretford End who was still king.

Any professional football man will testify to the greatness of Denis Law, who scored more goals for Scotland than any other man and who scored more FA Cup goals than any other man.

So too will a young old friend of mine, who was outside the profession of football, a well-educated young man and a football fanatic. But above all he was a Denis Law fanatic. Where Denis played so went my friend to watch him.

The day came for my young friend's wedding. In the hotel lift after the marriage ceremony he said to his bride: 'If you give me as much pleasure in the next ten years as Denis Law has given me in the last ten I am going to be the happiest married man in the world.'

At such a moment in such a place greater praise hath no man than this.

GEORGE BEST

Bob Bishop, a Manchester United scout in Northern Ireland, wrote to us to say that he had seen a young boy with an enormous ration of football gifts, though he had hesitated because the lad was so small and skinny.

'Send him over and let us have a look at him,' we said.

And George Best, with another wee lad, Eric McMordie, duly arrived.

Shortly afterwards, the senior players reported for the new season's call-up, were weighed and kitted up, completed the rest of the reporting-day chores and went home. In the afternoon I went along to see how the club's young players were going on. They were playing two-against-two and others of the training ploys. One black-haired little squib made a particular imprint on my mind.

Next day Master Best and Master McMordie came to see me at my office and said they wanted to go back home to Northern Ireland. They were homesick. I brought in Harry Gregg, our Northern Ireland goalkeeper, to try to influence them to stay. It did not work. So I said: 'All right, boys. You had better go home.'

The next week it kept coming back to me, the vision of this black-haired lad who had been doing such clever things with the ball. So I sat down and wrote to his father. I said I realized the boy was homesick but that I would be very happy if young George changed his mind and would be obliged if his father would send him back to Old Trafford if he did. About three weeks later I received a letter from Dick Best, the boy's father, saying that George would like another try.

It was not long before we realized what an astonishing little bundle of football's talents we had among us.

George Best was gifted with more individual ability than I have seen in any other player, certainly unique in the *number* of his gifts. He remained deceptively skinny-looking, but he was strong and courageous to a degree that compensated amply. He had more ways of beating a player than any other player I have seen. Every aspect of ball control was perfectly natural to him from the start. He even used his opponent's shins to his advantage by hitting the ball on to them so accurately that it came back to him like a one-two pass. He had more confidence in his own ability than I have seen in any other sportsman. He was always able to use either foot (sometimes he seemed to have six!). His heading was devastating. He was completely oblivious to pre-match tensions as I have said earlier. He was as unconcerned before a big match as he would be before a park kick-about.

He became certainly the best-known player in Britain and, with Pele, the best-known player in the world, which is remarkable since the Northern Ireland team in his time had made little World Cup impact. Never in football history has any other young man been so idolized by the young fraternity. His picture was on the walls of tens of thousands of kiddies' bedrooms all over the land. He became the biggest drawing power British football ever had.

I think it was quite naively at the time that he capitalized on the long-hair cult of the Beatles before the rest of the nation's youth caught on. Doubtless if he had changed to a short back-and-sides, so, too, would a million others, including hundreds of footballers with George Best hairdos.

On the pitch, if he had a fault in those younger days it was that he wanted to beat too many opponents when he could have passed the ball to better advantage. You would see him beat two or three or even four and then lose the ball and you would be having apoplectic fits and saying to yourself: 'Why the hell, George, don't you pass the ball?' Then he would beat two or three or even four more and score the winner. So what do you do about that? Such a player cannot be regimented.

Wherever he went, swarms of people enveloped him, friends, hangers-on, small boys, dear old ladies, and an inevitable gaggle of girls, who seemed to be attracted like moths to a light. I would have had to be blind and deaf not to be aware about some of the capers he got up to, or was rumoured to get up to, that were not within a footballer's accepted curriculum. I would have him up in my office and I would play the very devil with him. He did not hide this fact. John Morgan of the *Daily Express* quoted George thus: 'Don't let anyone kid you Sir Matt is soft. Every time I was in any sort of trouble – real or rumoured – he would send for me. I was in his office more often than *he* was. I had my own chair.'

Repeatedly I said to George: 'Why don't you find yourself a nice girl and get married?'

Once he met a girl in Scandinavia and soon after he returned the headlines bellowed: 'George Best to be married.' I could not get down to my office quickly enough. I had him in again. 'What's going on?' I said. 'What's all this about marrying a foreign girl you have only known a few weeks?'

113

And I went on to say why didn't he do like everybody else and marry someone a bit nearer home, someone he had known for some time? He could hardly wait for me to stop my lecture, and when I did eventually pause for breath he said: 'Aw boss, you're the one who's always telling me to get married.'

George Best, like Denis Law and many others, was given cruel treatment by some opponents. No player suffered more than he did in being chopped or hacked down. Such players would not have been in one quarter of the trouble they got themselves into on the pitch if they had been subjected to fair tackles all the time. But the answer by many mediocre players to brilliance is to hack it down. Only such victims know the frustrations and the provocation when brilliance is checked painfully by mediocrity. It is up to football to preserve the limbs of great players.

Best, like Law, had plenty of referee trouble, most often because of retaliation. It was after one of his brushes with authority that I went to London to speak for him at the disciplinary hearing. George did not turn up. It was an embarrassment to me and to the club. I have said that the job of a manager when he takes a boy under his wing is that he must in some ways be a father to him. I have always felt so.

But fathers everywhere will know that there are times when lads let down dads. All right, Johnny Morris of my first successful team, and Johnny Giles later, were transferred out, and they had not embarrassed me in this way. But Morris and Giles *asked* to go. George Best and I did not disagree. He knew perfectly well that he was letting me down every time he let himself down and let the club down. And he always apologized.

We fined him. We suspended him. What more could we do? We couldn't shoot him. We might have felt like smacking his bottom, as a man might smack his own son's bottom. But this is not allowed in a player's contract. After one of his mad moments I had him in my office again and I said: 'Why don't you come and live at my home for a while? Just until you get yourself sorted out.' I told him he would have the freedom of the house and as much privacy as he wanted. Obviously he would feel under some sort of obligation to discipline himself. He turned this idea down.

But it is important that the boy underneath the man Best

114

should not be condemned out of hand for his indiscretions, or made out to be a hard-boiled, no-good, unappreciative, spoiled brat. It may or may not surprise people to know that George Best broke down and cried once after I ticked him off, ashamed that he had let me and the club down, by then possibly suffering from some of the extreme tensions that grew year by year around him, and which eventually went near to strangling him psychologically.

So George was one of the legacies I handed over to Frank O'Farrell.

And about a year later, the front page and back page of the newspapers were full of George Best. I am not proud of this. Nor is George, I am sure. But it is quite incredible that a footballer could virtually monopolize the British press as he did when he declared in an article that he would not play football again. After which he did not turn up to play for Northern Ireland and he did not turn up to play with Manchester United in Israel. His 'crimes' as far as Manchester United were concerned were that he had written the article without permission and that he had not turned up for the match in Israel.

The Press followed him around the sunny beaches of Spain until he came back to Old Trafford cured, temporarily at least, of whatever ailment he had. As Joe Mercer once said: 'Football could live without me but I couldn't live without football.' So it seemed to be with George.

Experts, most of them not in the game but some who were, said that in Frank O'Farrell's place they would have thrown George out. We at Manchester United were always looking for a *cure*. It *was* Frank O'Farrell's responsibility. As I say, George Best was a problem legacy. Many experts in the game would like such a problem.

George Best never did anything wrong at Old Trafford under my management without being punished for it, with the directors' approval, and invariably he apologized. But if this outburst *had* come when he was still under my jurisdiction I would not have bowed to the clamour for his head. I know that George Best underneath is a good, generous, kindly lad. I think he found himself in the wrong company in his young, formative years. I do not say *bad* company. I mean the wrong company at a time when he should have been looking around for a wife. The adulation must have

115

been a problem once the novelty wore off. Girls virtually flung themselves at him. So he had his silly moments. But always he would come back and be the perfect professional again, because then he was always in love with his training.

It was at the end of the 1971-2 season that he made his outburst in the Press. George Best and Manchester United had had a great first half of the season. We were five points in front of the nearest challenger. Then he lost his form, and what looked like lack of interest by George seemed to affect the whole team, though I would not put all the blame on Best. Whatever the reason, we had a poor second half of a season in which we had looked set for the championship.

Just as Denis Law had always said: 'I can't promise I won't hit back if I am kicked', there was no way of knowing about the future of George Best under the same stresses plus other stresses nobody except George could really know about.

I did not believe his indiscretions would be cured by saying: 'You have finished with Manchester United.' He was still young, still in some ways immature. Some of the immense pressures he brought on himself. He ran away from problems instead of facing them. But I set great store by patience. We had to hope that he would be cured, this the greatest entertainer, the world's most gifted player, who, man and boy, filled football grounds wherever he played and made people gasp and laugh by his sheer audacity.

Football is not so wealthy in its talents that it can spare such a genius – and if ever there was a football genius George Best is that player, a man uniquely gifted for football. I have to confess that though George Best was no longer my responsibility I still had fatherly instincts for the boy I tempted away from his Irish home despite his homesickness, and who brought pain but greater rewards to me, as most boys bring great pain and even greater joy to their parents.

A man does not give up sons who love him as he loves them – unless they are determined to leave the nest.

If the boy is sick, a father doesn't kick him out. He hopes for a cure.

But, sadly, late in 1972, George said, for the second time, that he would not play football again. What the future held for George Best then, who could tell?

116

PART THREE

THE GREATS—PAST AND PRESENT

WHAT IS GREATNESS?

I believe I have influenced people in my long life in football. I do not suggest that any player or manager has consciously copied me. Experience means not only lessons learned from mistakes. It also means a collection of worthwhile information quite subconsciously pigeonholed in the brainbox, from talking to or watching others with something to say or to show. So although I have not copied any man my football thinking has been influenced by close contact with great men from my boyhood.

I was as football daft as any of the boys in the village of Bellshill, and dafter than most, and we had our idols already. There were two young fellows called Alex James and Hughie Gallacher, for instance. They would be about eighteen or nineteen, I suppose, I about nine or ten. They were little whippets as footballers go, but they were famous. Why, everybody in Bellshill, knew what players they were! They played at the time for two juvenile teams in the area, juvenile meaning teams in lower status than the Scottish League but brimful of the best young players in the villages who had not, or not yet, reached the big game.

I was still at school, of course, but I was hamper boy to James's team, humping kit, and generally helping and fussing about. I do not know why, but something went wrong with Alex James's boots, or they were missing, and the great man borrowed my football boots. I was a big boy and he was a little man. Soon the village knew about it. I proclaimed it to all my friends or whoever was in earshot. 'Alex James played in my boots!' It will have been noticed that I proclaim it still, and that is because, as young as I was and as small and insignificant though little Bellshill might seem in the big world of football, I saw magic in those early days, the magic of two of the greatest footballers in the game's history in one small village.

Magic because even then James used to mesmerize his opponents with a feint that said: 'Now I'm here, now I'm not', and Gallacher used to paralyse them with a dribbling run and power of shot and a line of pertinent or impertinent patter to go with it.

James went on to become football's king of England after leaving Preston North End for Arsenal. They talk today about middle men as if they were a modern invention. In the magnificent Arsenal of the early Thirties James was the great creator from the middle. From an Arsenal rearguard action the ball would, seemingly inevitably, reach Alex. He would feint and leave two or three opponents sprawling or plodding in his wake before he released the ball, unerringly, to either the flying Joe Hulme, who would not even have to pause in his flight, or the absolutely devastating Cliff ('Boy') Bastin, who would take a couple of strides and whip the ball into the net. The number of goals created from rearguard beginnings by Alex James were the most significant factor in Arsenal's greatness.

I played against James and Gallacher in their later but still great days, after Gallacher had left Newcastle United for Chelsea. I was a nobody, but they remembered the boy who had looked after the hamper and always had words of encouragement for me, their opponent now, with a welcome 'Well done, son,' or 'Well played, Matt.' Not that this in any way deterred them from leaving me sitting on my bottom with the rest.

Alex James sent more opponents 'into the tube station' with a little feint than any other man who ever shook a hip. I remember a couple of wags shouting to me before a match in which the great Alex was in the opposition. One of them bawled out: 'Don't worry, Matt, we've just locked James in the toilet.' (Spectators didn't use naughty words in those days.) Gallacher seemed unrobbable. If the ball had been tied to his boots with string it could not have been more adhesive. Incidentally, James and Gallacher took as much stick from tough nut defenders as any modern 'great' does. I saw their bruises.

It will seem, after all this gush about two of the old masters, that sentiment, or nostalgia, has the better of me, and that I have fallen into the old trap of saying that the greats are in the past, like ghosts, reappearing in the memory, and that greatness is gone forever.

But had I at any time fallen into such a trap how could I

have had implicit faith in my own brainchild, the youth policy that served me so well? The point I insist on is that greatness is not confined to any age or any country but is a matter of gifts, genetics, and I also insist that present-day arguments which take the line that the greats of yesterday would not live in the game today are as silly as those which go to the opposite extreme.

Greatness, like truth, will out. James, Gallacher and others I will mention had all the gifts of greatness, and, whatever training techniques had been used with them, whatever defensive techniques had been used against them, their inherent difference from ordinary players would have made them stand out. Past or present, all players who get into Football League teams, have exceptional skill. After all there are only a few thousand of them at one time out of a population of fifty million. They are discovered and trained by professional experts and they are constantly in opposition to professional experts, which is the best practice of all. So the average quality is high. But today's ordinary players are more useful than yesterday's because they are made to run farther and faster and for longer. This has made it more difficult for the great player to look great, because almost always if a man is beaten he has another and another and another to cover him.

Circumstances will change the game again and yet again, as one strategy is countered successfully and another is tried. But whatever changes come and however destructive the strategy the great will out as they always did.

Greatness is doing things that are different, things the ordinary player cannot do. But each great player is different too, so it is really of little use comparing one great player with another. I believe it is reasonable to say that A and B were both great, but it can only be a personal opinion to say that A was greater than B. Take Alex James and George Best. Both great footballers – everybody who saw both play must agree with that. It can only be a matter of opinion to say which was greater, especially since they played at different times, but not only *because* they played at different times, since it is still a matter of opinion to say that one contemporary was greater than another, say Tom Finney than Stan Matthews (we will go into that argument later), or Charlton than Beckenbauer.

DIXIE DEAN

Who could ever have seen Bill (Dixie) Dean and not seen greatness? My first sight of him was when I first arrived in Manchester to join City as a boy of seventeen. He was playing for Everton against Manchester United at Old Trafford. He confirmed what I had heard. He scored a hat-trick. So this was English football. So this was Dixie Dean. Oh dear!

To play against Dixie Dean was at once a delight and a nightmare. He was a perfect specimen of an athlete, beautifully proportioned, with immense strength, adept on the ground but with extraordinary skill in the air. However close you watched him, his timing in the air was such that he was coming down before you got anywhere near him, and he hit that ball with his head as hard and as accurately as most players could kick it. Defences were close to panic when corners came over. And though he scored a huge tally of goals with headers he was an incredibly unselfish and amazingly accurate layer-off of chances for others. He was resilient in face of the big, tough centre-halves of his day – and I cannot think of one centre-half today to match up with that lot, though it was often the unstoppable force against the immovable object – and he was a thorough sportsman.

Dixie scored a record sixty League goals in the season 1927-8 in thirty-nine games, plus three FA Cup goals and nineteen in representative games, for a total of eighty-two. There cannot be another Dixie Dean any more than there can be another anybody else. If there could be the new Dixie would still score a great pile of goals. He would out-jump, out-time, out-head any defender or any number they could pack into the area. As a header of the ball only Denis Law and, less often, since he was more at the back than the front, Jack Charlton have come within a mile of Dixie.

FINNEY AND MATTHEWS

Greatness can be a magical quality. The joy of seeing it is the joy of seeing something remarkable, say, George Best using an opponent's shin to rebound the ball to him as if it were a colleague indulging in the old one-two wall pass, a hesitation step by Alex James that would have an opponent floundering all over the place, a come-and-get-me invitation look by Stan Matthews until the poor opponent came and was left conquered and cork-legged, a left-footed Tom Finney going down the right wing in full flight.

And there I have mentioned two names that have caused more arguments among football supporters than any other top two in England. I wouldn't mind betting there have been more debates in English pubs after somebody has said: 'Who is greater, Finney or Matthews?' than about any General Election.

The only similarities between Matthews and Finney are that both were great and both were murder to play against. No man can say who was the greater, and it is with some trepidation that I venture some opinions about them. First, to those who say that if Stan Matthews, who played League football until he was fifty, and who became Sir Stanley for his services to football, were to be young again and play today, he would not be as great as he was, I have to say: 'Nonsense.' I will then be challenged that Stan would not go back to full-back as soon as the ball is kicked off as all wingers seem to do these days. I will then say that Stan Matthews would need only to stay up front to cause half the opposition to stay back with him.

I speak with some knowledge. I had the doubtful pleasure of playing against Stanley Matthews and the real pleasure of playing with him for the combined services. He would come to you with the ball at his dainty feet. He would take you on. You had seen it all before. You knew precisely what he would do and you knew precisely what he would do with you. He would pass you, usually on the outside, but as a novelty on the inside. If you went to tackle him it was merely saving time for him. He then simply beat you. If you didn't he would tease you by coming straight up to you and showing you the ball. And that would be the last you would see of him in that move. If you were covered he would do the same with your cover man and his cover man and so ad infinitum. Then, in his own good time and not before, he would release the perfect pass.

In his moments he would tear a man apart, tear a team apart. He might not be in it for three-quarters of the game. In the other quarter he would destroy you. He wasn't in it in his winning Cup Final for Blackpool against Bolton Wanderers in 1953 for much that mattered until the last phase, during which he destroyed Bolton and laid on the victory. He usually laid everything on for others to finish off. No amount of cover would have stopped him in his magical moments. People were as aware of him as they are of any player today. They set out to stop him as they set out to stop the best today. But the best can't be stopped just by setting people on them.

Stan Matthews was basically a right-footed player, Tom Finney a left-footed player, though Tom's right was as good as most players' better foot. Matthews gave the ball only when he was good and ready and the move was ripe to be finished off. Finney was more of a team player, Matthews being more of an inspiration to a team than a single part of it. Finney was more inclined to join in moves and build them up with colleagues, by giving and taking back. He would beat a man with a pass or with wonderful individual runs that left the opposition in disarray. And Finney would also finish the whole thing off by scoring, which Stan seldom did. Being naturally left-footed, Tom was absolutely devastating on the right wing. An opponent never seemed to be able to get at him. If you were a problem to him he had two solutions for you.

Tom Finney could and would and did play in any forward position. Like Stan Matthews he was never in any trouble with referees. Stan was knighted after his immense period as a player. Tom was awarded the OBE. I do not say that Tom should have played until he was fifty. I do say that I was sorry he did not play for two or three years more than he did, even though he was in his late thirties.

How can anybody say who was the greater? I think I would choose Matthews for the big occasion – he played as if he was playing the Palladium. I would choose Finney, the lesser showman but still a beautiful sight to see, for the greater impact on his team. For moments of magic – Matthews. For immense versatility – Finney. Coming down to an all-purpose selection about whom I would choose for my side if I could have one or the other I would choose Finney. Now I await cries of 'Rubbish!'

Will any two moderns cause so many arguments? Possibly, possibly not. But if proper wingers come back from banishment great ones will certainly emerge. George Best will cause as many arguments, even if not arguments in comparing him with a single other player. And George might be called a winger. Otherwise I do not think wingers have emerged in the Matthews-Finney class, probably because none of them has been allowed enough practise at it. But they *will* emerge.

JIMMY McMULLAN

They used to say: Tell me your half-back line and I will tell you your team. The half-back line was the source from which all blessings flowed. They used the same middle of the park which has of recent years been mentioned as if it were a new extension to the pitch. The trouble after 1966 was that they stuck anybody and everybody in the middle of the park, where half of them were merely bodies and legs like a dozen goalposts in a single goal. Most of them had not a really creative move in their heads, or the craft to provide it if they had.

In the time of Alex James and Hughie Gallacher was another wee Scot, also in the Wee Blue Devils team that thrashed England at Wembley. He was Jimmy McMullan, the Manchester City captain, a magician of a wing-half, who was an amazing passer of the ball and a superb tactician. The McMullans were very kind to me when I first moved to England. They took me into their home and were one of the big reasons why I stayed in England at all. Compare him with some of the 'ball-winners' of today and the comparison is laughable. Would he have been any good today? The great passer of a ball will get in any team today.

JIMMY GREAVES

As pretty a little player as I ever did see, and, apart from Denis Law, the most lethal finisher in the penalty box, was little Jimmy Greaves. No matter what the goalmouth scramble, the nimble, perfectly-balanced Jimmy would seem to find himself room for a ballet-dancer's pivot, and in a flash there would be the lift of that tiny left foot and the ball would be glided into the net. He did everything crisply, neatly. He could lose defenders by stealth and psychic game-reading. He took the ball-player's lion's share of the rough stuff without complaint, though he had the knack of placing himself away from it and had the facility for making the offender look like a big clumsy oaf, which was not his intention, because gentleman Jimmy Greaves had not an ounce of venom in him. Typically he drifted out of the game with no great noise. I wish he had stayed longer.

BOBBY MOORE

Few great players get themselves into a lather, few seem to be in a hurry, even in international football. I do not think it generally appreciated that there *is* an immense difference between international football and even the First Division of Football League, which is the next highest I can think of in terms of demands on players. Some otherwise great players never quite overcome the complex that taxes their confidence in their first international game. They cannot play their own skilful game for thinking how great everybody else on the pitch is. So they hurry things; they let themselves down. But some players are born international class. Such a man is Bobby Moore.

Some silly spectators, particularly in the North – because of a natural North *v.* South supporters' vendetta – gave Bobby the barracking treatment, and did so purely and simply because his game was so consistently great. They looked for his every slip and then let him have it. It is nonsense, but football spectating is an emotional business, and I have never yet heard a convincing explanation for it. The effect of such barracking on Bobby Moore was nil. He got on with his game quite impervious to anything else but the next move. Before long he had them, barrackers and all, however reluctantly, applauding him.

One of the annoying things for opposing supporters is that Bobby Moore seems to have so much time and space at his disposal. The ball seems to be magnetically attracted to him. The reason for this is that he can see which way the game is going to go while the ball is still eighty yards away.

It is called reading the game, and I do believe it cannot be explained unless clairvoyance has something to do with it. I don't think it can be taught. Bobby Moore's play looks effortless but it is not so effortless as it looks. He has carried a load of responsibility, to himself because of his well-earned reputation, to his team because he has been captain, and it is not possible to be captain of a more important team than the one that wins the World Cup as England did under Bobby in 1966.

There are many more geniuses in Britain's football history. I apologise for not including them. The few I have mentioned merely typify both the greatness and the differences, and show that no decade has a corner on genius. There are football geniuses among us today and will be to-morrow. Will Kevin Keegan of Liverpool qualify? Will Trevor Francis, Alan Hudson, Mike Channon, Colin Todd? And will Tony Currie? His playing style reminds me of the great German, Netzer.

GOALKEEPERS: HIBBS; SWIFT; TRAUTMANN; BANKS; SHILTON

I am surprised that goalkeepers don't form a club. They are a race apart, because goalkeeping is a different game from the rest of football, as putting is a different game from the rest of golf. A golfer can play the most incredibly difficult shots brilliantly and nullify the lot with the daftest of little putts. A team can play the most brilliant football, score three goals, and lose 4–3 because the goalkeeper has made only one mistake in a match in which everybody else has made half a dozen apiece. It is not surprising, with this awful responsibility, that the saying goes that all goalkeepers are mad. I never met a mad goalkeeper, but, as (I hope) a fairly sane person I would never have chucked myself into some of the free-for-all scrimmages most goalkeepers face as an accepted part of their job.

Football teams, I have always thought, have two bastions – the goalkeeper and the centre-half. If you have a good defence but a bad goalkeeper you are in trouble. If you have a bad defence and a good goalkeeper you might get away with it. It is the same with centre-halves.

The big goalkeeper of my earlier days in England was a small one as goalkeepers go. Yet Harry Hibbs, of Birmingham, made goalkeeping look as easy as Beckenbauer made upfield play look, and for the same reason. Harry put himself in the right places. He seldom had to dive around to have the ball. He always seemed to be standing exactly where the shot happened to be going. There was no fuss, there were few aerobatics, no recriminations.

Then there was a young fellow I knew from his very beginnings in the League. He played for Manchester City and his his name was Frank Swift, or, to the fraternity, Big Swifty, one of the greatest and certainly the most cheerful characters I have come across in a game which, in the grim, unsmiling days of the Seventies, could do with a few like him. Swifty was a mere boy when he played with me in City's winning Cup Final against Portsmouth in 1934. The occasion proved too much for him and at the end of it he fainted. Trying to pull himself together in the dressing room afterwards he stammered: 'Have we won?'

Many years later, talking to a friend of mine, Frank told of the time when he was very young, playing for City against Birmingham. Alec Herd took a free kick from thirty yards out and the ball was in the net before the great Harry Hibbs could move. At the end of the game, as they went off together, the boy Swift said to the master Hibbs: 'What happened with Alec's free kick?' – and the great man said: 'If you can't see 'em, son, you can't stop 'em.'

Big Swifty fainted only once in a dressing room. He developed into the cheeriest dressing-room man in the game of football, whether playing for Manchester City or England. In any company he was a brilliant raconteur. In the dressing room his infectious good humour brought a smile to even the most nervous beginner.

On the pitch he was the first showman goalkeeper. But first he was a magnificent goalkeeper, *second* a showman. He believed in entertaining the crowd. He played with a smile and with banter to match. Some opponent would send in a mighty shot. The big hands of Big Swifty would envelop it as if it had been a gentle lob. 'Good shot, that, Joe,' he would say to the man who had cracked it in. No matter who was captain there was only one boss in Swifty's goalmouth. It went without saying, though he said it often enough: 'If I shout, get out of my way. If you don't I'll knock you out of the way.' He was the first goalkeeper I saw who threw the ball out, accurately and over great distances, to a colleague, instead of merely punting it up the pitch and giving the other team an equal chance of getting it. He would pick it up one-handed and throw it like a cricket ball.

For a big man, Swifty was phenomenally agile. He narrowed the angle for an opponent to shoot in as if he had made a science of it. His showmanship was not exhibitionism. He wanted to demonstrate that football could include a bit of fun, a quality sadly missing from the game today. He was immensely popular everywhere he played, as popular with opposition and opposition suporters as with his own team and his own team's supporters. If any footballer could be termed lovable, Big Swifty was the man.

But there was just one occasion when I wished him miles away from me. He was playing for England, I for Scotland, before about 125,000 people at Hampden Park, Glasgow. We had played together for Manchester City for years. We knew each other's play with a familiarity born of hours and years of practice together and many, many matches together. We Scots had discussed who should take penalty kicks, and though I did not want to take them we decided I should do so.

At the height of interest in the match, when England were leading 3-1 but Scotland were well on top and striving desperately to reduce the lead, we were awarded a penalty. Here I would like to say a word or two about taking penalty kicks. The generally accepted view of people who never have to take them is that a professional footballer should never miss one, and that if he does he should (a) have his wages stopped, (b) be sacked or (c) be shot. After all, the penalty spot is only twelve yards from the goal. The goalkeeper is not allowed to move until the taker has taken the kick. And your target measures eight yards by eight feet.

Somehow it does not seem all that easy when you are the one delegated to take the kick. It is not too bad if you are already about 5-1 with fifteen minutes to go. You can stride nonchalantly up to the ball, take a casual whack at it, and ninety-nine times out of a hundred it goes precisely where you want it to go. But if it is a vital penalty the whole operation takes on a different aspect. It takes on an *extremely* different aspect if you are taking a penalty kick for Scotland, with 100,000 Scots, who are apt to take a match against England with some seriousness, waiting to let you know, if you are so stupid as to miss it, what they think of you, especially if you would be only a goal behind if you scored with it.

Any penalty kick taker will confirm that on such vital occasions the goalkeeper looks bigger, the goal looks shorter and narrower, your heart beats faster, and your knees knock louder. The shot itself is not a simple place-it-and-kick-it business. Some chaps like to place the shot, some like to blast it. I was one of those clever fellows who like to show their skill by placing it into one corner or the other. My problem was Frank Swift. I had taken a thousand penalty kicks against him at practice. He knew my style. He knew where I liked to place them, and where I almost always tried to place them.

It seems impossible as I set this down that all the thoughts that went through my mind did so as I took the short walk to place the ball, the few steps back, and the run-up to kick it. Shall I place the ball to Frank's left, since he will be expecting it to go, as usual, to his right? On the other hand, I cogitated, he might well say to himself: 'I know Matt, he will try to kid me by putting it to my left side, so I will dive left.' (I hardly need to explain that a goalkeeper has to make up his mind and take the fifty-fifty chance and dive one way or the other. There is no time to cogitate once the taker has taken the penalty kick.) But then, I thought, Frank will guess that I have seen through his reasoning and he will see through mine and he will dive to his right. Anyway, I put it to his right.

Frank dived, and saved it.

There was a groan from 100,000 Scottish throats, a cheer from 25,000 English ones, then a great low, grumbling noise as of people telling their fellows where one player ought to go and that player was Matt Busby. So although I am all for the niceties, although I am all for the polish and style, and have no great passion for the crash-bashers of the game, I strongly recommend, especially if the goalkeeper has had plenty of practice against you, to give that ball a mighty whack at goal, in Francis Lee's style for Manchester City. Not that every player can whack the ball as hard as Francis.

At Hampden that day I wished Frank Swift, my old pal, was far away. But just as the finest penalty kickers sometimes miss them, the finest goalkeepers sometimes let sloppy shots go in, usually because the ball has hit a divot, or the keeper has lost concentration for a moment, or he had expected a hard one, dived, and the ball bobbled slowly over his prostrate body into the net.

I was with Big Swifty from his beginnings in League football. And I was with him when he died at Munich. He was only forty-three. He died when he had much fun still in him to share with friends, neighbours and strangers.

When Frank Swift retired, Manchester City supporters felt there was a gap that could not be filled. How could any other goalkeeper give them such brilliance, such skill, such fun? None could give them all these things. Because like all other footballers all goalkeepers, including great goalkeepers, are different. But, astonishingly, suddenly and soon, City had another superman, a former German prisoner of war, one Bernhard Carl Trautmann, hereinafter given his more homely Lancashire name of Bert. Speaking with feeling, I cannot count the number of times the extraordinary Trautmann came to Manchester City's rescue against Manchester United, during a period when United were consistently a fair number of classes better than City. A tall man, like Swift, but not so gangly, Trautmann was a magnificent specimen. He was as agile as Frank, and his handling was as sure. The ball seemed to be magnetized to him. His reflexes were so sharp that he could dive one way and stretch an arm back in mid-air and make a save that had seemed impossible.

He must have been heartbreaking for marksmen. An opponent would take a most tremendous swipe at the ball, it would go like a bullet something like head high, and Trautmann would, with the utmost calm, catch it in front of his face as if a child had thrown a tennis ball to him. Imagine the frustration of the player who hit a ball which almost any other keeper would have had to punch away or palm away, to see the great man take it as if it were a dolly drop. It was enough to make him weep. Swift and Trautmann covered a period of about thirty years for Manchester

City. I doubt that any club anywhere has been served with such class in this position for so long a spell.

Who can say which one was the greater? Who can say that either was greater than Gordon Banks, first for Leicester City and England, then for Stoke City and England? Gordon had every quality a goalkeeper could have, including almost psychic anticipation and lightning reflexes that made some of his saves border on the miraculous, a facility, indeed, for stopping the seemingly unstoppable. And curiously, in another remarkable horses-for-courses sequence, Leicester City had in Gordon's successor a man who also looked like his natural successor in the England team, Peter Shilton, though he has a little way to go to match the seemingly matchless Banks.

I have seen many, many magnificent goalkeepers. I have merely mentioned the greatest in my estimation. As for all goalkeepers being mad, if a man has to be mad to be brave I might concede it. Goalkeepers have to be brave.

OVERSEAS MASTERS

In thinking of the wider, European scene, I never saw a greater all-round player than Alfredo di Stefano, the Argentinian who was outstanding even for Real Madrid at their peak. His work-rate was phenomenal – the nearest thing to perpetual motion. Not surprisingly di Stefano once said: 'I need 48 hours to get over a match.'

When I recall the speed and power of Gento and the agility and nimble left foot of the portly Puskas I am excited even at the memory of them. 'He's very left-footed,' said a sceptical Scot of Puskas, to which his neighbour replied: 'It's a guid job he hasnae two like it or we'd be in a recht bloody mess.'

Who could fail to be entranced by the nobility of Franz Beckenbauer's football for West Germany, or the almost incredible skills of Pele, the Brazilian, football's king from boyhood, an outstanding goal-scorer and goal-maker even in the world class? Unless goal-scoring is made easier nobody will equal his goal tally of more than 1,000. How lucky we are who are privileged to have seen him.

PART FOUR

MANAGERS—THE FIRING LINE

WHAT MAKES A MANAGER?

The best footballers do not necessarily make the best managers. It is even closer to the facts to say that great players seldom make successful managers. The technical gifts that make a footballer great have little in common with the gifts that make for managership and indeed they may constitute actual drawbacks for good managership. The instinctive, prolifically-gifted player is apt to take his gifts for granted and to wonder why his colleagues do not respond to his instincts or why they do not, indeed, have the same instincts. Since his tricks almost always succeed, he does not need to occupy his time wondering why not and what can he do to improve the trick that did not work. If he happens to be a great player with also a cannonball shot, which is by no means a necessary corollary to greatness, he can no more inspire less gifted players to send in cannonball shots than can the most learned anatomical or ballistic theorist.

When his playing career is done the great player is no more capable of putting over his case as a manager, unless he is one of the few prodigiously gifted characters who have succeeded in being great players *and* great managers, than he was as a player. He still wonders why the men in his charge cannot do the things he did as a matter of course. And since he has not had to struggle to improve, he is unlikely to be an expert in showing ordinary players how to improve their play within the limitations of their gifts. Here I should stress that *all* players who reach Football League status, since they are the best few thousand in a population of fifty million, *have* gifts, just as there are tremendously gifted man in all walks of life who fall short of genius. Nor in any walk of life are geniuses often the best communicators. So our great player who becomes a manager carries an aura of arrogance, making use of the overworked admonishment: 'I am not asking you to do anything I cannot do myself.'

Managers, like footballers, are a motley lot, with no two alike except in the agony they go through. I am not referring here to the agony of wondering if you are the next one for the sack. The sack is an occupational hazard. I do not care what system football is suffering from at any time on the field of play, some team still finishes bottom, and that means, very often, exit manager.

HERBERT CHAPMAN

Men of stature really have their own effect on football by doing something different when something different is needed. The sheep follow, until some other man of stature leads them along a different path his adventurous, probing mind has charted. Such an adventurer was Herbert Chapman, who in transforming Arsenal transformed the game of football.

Chapman was an adventurer who had caution as his watchword. I do not mean that he was cautious with money – well not with Arsenal's money at any rate. He took Huddersfield Town to two successive championships and then in 1925 joined Arsenal, whereupon he paid Sunderland £2,000 plus £100 per goal for Charlie Buchan, who proceeded to score twenty-one goals that season, nineteen in the League, two in the Cup, and Arsenal were beaten for the championship only by Huddersfield, who thereby made it a hat-trick of titles.

That was adventurous enough, and so it was when Chapman lashed out the considerable fees for those days of nearly £11,000 for Bolton Wanderers' David Jack, and £9,000 for Preston North End's Alex James. But the most revolutionary move was the cheapest and simplest. Chapman (using an idea of Buchan's, it was said) evolved the third-back game around the solid Herbie Roberts, and thus ended the roving commission and the more adventurous play of centre-halves. The gentleman with the No 5 on his back became thereafter a stopper rather than a stopper-starter-wanderer, almost stationary in the middle of the backs or behind them.

The idea, wildly exaggerated now by adding a few more backs, was patently to keep at least the point you start off with. That was the cautious Chapman. The other clubs throughout the game, sooner or later, followed suit. Their problem was that they hadn't an Alex James, a David Jack, a Cliff Bastin or a Joe Hulme, to name only four, and I have said my piece about the James man and the James plan.

Chapman bought the players to suit his ideas. He was more a visionary than a coach. If he wasn't a coach as modern coaches go he had what could be more use to some modern coaches than their obsession with numbers and plans. He was inspiring. He was persuasive. He could persuade a player how he could be the greatest at a certain job. He persuaded Alex James to be the great provider from the middle.

Herbert Chapman died in 1934, but the results of his inspiring leadership and his building are shown by Arsenal's five championships between 1930 and 1938 (three in succession) and their FA Cup wins in 1930 and 1936. Those who followed him were bound to be haunted by his ghost.

DON REVIE

The third-back game stayed with us. Although it smacked of caution, it was efficient, and it seemed to be here for ever. But measures in football inevitably bring counter-measures, and one day we were all brought down to earth from the safety of our third-back haven by the Hungarians, who used Hidegkuti, a centre-forward (or a man wearing No 9) playing in the deep with Puskas and Kocsis up ready to pounce on the passes he played up to them.

Now it was all very well setting your centre-half in the middle to cope with the big, strong, bustling centre-forward of the opposition. Sometimes it was the immovable versus the unstoppable, although the centre-half had the advantage, inasmuch as he was almost always facing the ball, whereas the centre-forward almost always, if he had the ball, was forced to turn round with it. But the centre-half facing *two* centre-forwards literally did not know which way to turn. If he moved to Kocsis the deep-lying Hidegkuti

136

would play the ball to Puskas, or vice versa. England were undone. Wembley blushed to see Hungary win 6-3.

About a year later, Manchester City, peering round in the mists of their mediocrity, began to startle everybody by trying a facsimile of the Hungarian plan. Their manager, Les McDowall, always a serious student of the game, having tried the idea with the reserves, played Don Revie in a deep-lying centre-forward role. I call it a reduced facsimile of the Hungarians because, good goal-getters and good professionals though they were, nobody would put Johnny Hart and Joe Hayes, for instance, in the Kocsis-Puskas class, but Joe and Johnny were two of those who exploited Don Revie's splendid interpretation of the Hidegkuti plan to which Don's accurate long passing and his brilliance with the chipped ball were ideally suited.

Two sharp marksmen like Joe Hayes and Johnny Hart were just what Doctor Revie ordered. And I have to say that others played their part in the Revie Plan, including the magnificent Welsh international captain, Roy Paul.

Don Revie made the Revie Plan and, I am sure he would concede, the Revie Plan made Don Revie. Don began as a fine, dedicated professional footballer. He was first with Leicester City, moved to Hull City in 1949 for about £20,000, and then went to Manchester City in 1951 for about £25,000 – these were big fees for the time. But not until the 1954-5 season, when the invention of the Revie Plan displayed his creative genius with the long ball, did he become a household name. City reached the 1955 Cup Final and lost to Newcastle United and the next year went to Wembley again and beat Birmingham City. It was the happiest post-war spell for City until Joe Mercer arrived.

The first of Don's England caps came in 1955. Later he was transferred to Sunderland and then to Leeds United, who were relegated to the Second Division at the end of the 1959-60 season, and were in no shape to win anything.

At the same time that Leeds were looking round for a manager in 1961, Harry Reynolds, a director, sent a letter off recommending Don Revie as player-manager of Bournemouth. Harry was often heard to say: 'I know nowt about football,' but he showed he knew a lot about people. As soon as he had posted the letter he said to himself: 'What have I done? This is the very man for us!' He recommended Don to the board, who thereupon appointed him as player-manager, and Leeds United had made the best move in their history, in which they had had many great players but had never won anything important.

Not long after this Don asked to see me. The reason was simple enough. He wanted advice, something we can all do with from time to time. I was happy to help because I could see at once that he had many of the attributes needed. The very fact that he had taken the trouble to come to see me at all showed that thoroughness was one of them. Obviously he thought that if he could learn something of the snags he might do something to avoid them rather than wait and learn *everything* from bitter experience. On the other hand he seemed alive to situations and to have a good idea how to handle them. Of course, he had been a bit of a nomad as a player and he had learned a thing or two about players and managers and directors en route.

I saw that Don was a shrewd, firm character as well as a straight one, and I liked something else I saw. He was an *intense* character, bursting to start building and to justify himself, bursting to succeed. Therefore I could see he was willing to give. I saw that he would sweat it out as he would insist that his players would sweat it out.

Don was shrewd enough to recognize that he needed a right arm and a left arm, and a shoulder to lean on. He appointed staunch men of energy, drive, fire and technical skill. Maurice Lindley, Syd Owen, Les Cocker and others were all as different as different could be, both different from himself and from each other, except in the burning desire to build something that Leeds could be proud of. If called upon they would suffer for each other. Such men a manager needs. Without them the greatest technician, the most astute brain, the loudest talker, the most discreet diplomat, even a combination of all four, cannot succeed in a game that threatens to kill you once per week and twice per week at some parts of the season.

So Don Revie extracted every ounce from his players too, and Leeds United became one of the great names in Europe. I would be less than honest if I said I had agreed with some of their tactics on the pitch at times along their way to huge success. Some of them were foreign to Don's own style as a player.

I have been vastly impressed by the efficiency, the enormous skill of Billy Bremner and Johnny Giles, the versatility of Jack Charlton at front *and* rear, the craftsmanship and effort of all others. Prizes talk for themselves, and Don's men have won plenty of those. Under Revie, Leeds won the First Division in 1968-9; were runners-up 1964-5, 1965-6, 1969-70, 1970-1. Second Division Champions 1963-4, FA Cupwinners 1971-2, runners-up 1964-5, 1969-70, Football League Cupwinners 1967-8, European Fairs Cupwinners 1967-8, 1970-1, Finalists 1966-7. I am proud of Manchester United's prizes. Don and Leeds are fully entitled to be proud of theirs.

BRIAN CLOUGH

That empty kettles make most noise, or as I prefer it, the louder the dafter, I have found to be generally true in football and outside it. Generally, but not always. Two of the younger and louder managers have proved exceptions, Malcolm Allison is one. Brian Clough is the other. Like Malcolm, he showed that he was no mere bag of wind by hauling Derby County from Second Division obscurity to the First Division Championship in five years. He did it by using his excellent judgement in signing players and inspiring them to be better players, by building to a pattern that suited them, by encouraging them to play entertaining, progressive football, and not stooping to violence.

In his unhappily short (eight years) playing career, curtailed in his prime, at twenty-nine, by an injury, he was one of the most prolific goalscorers in football, reaching a remarkable tally of 250 or more, most of them for Middlesbrough, whom he later left to join Sunderland. Goodness knows how many he would have tallied if he could have played on. True, his goals were scored in the Second Division, and we shall never know whether he would have scored so many in the First Division, though he played twice for England, and he *did* score five in one match for the Football League against the Irish League, which may or may not be a criterion.

On the other hand it is a great pity that a player of Brian Clough's quality was fated to play only a few games in the

First Division. It must have been a constant source of frustration for him. Perhaps this is the source of some of the lamentations that poured from his lips when he became a manager, lamentations not of self-pity but about other people and other people's performances and attitudes.

It could be that his sing-song speech, which sounded, indeed, like a lament without the bagpipes, made his words sound more sneering than they were. But whereas Malcolm Allison's forthright statements made people laugh, Brian Clough's made many of them cringe, or so a great number of people have told me. Some of them made *me* cringe anyway. He said he liked airing his views on the television. That was all right for him. He didn't have to watch and listen, and when football is being talked who wants to switch off?

It was a pity. Because some of the things Brian Clough said needed to be said. Nobody with any sense would say a manager who won the League Championship did not know what he was talking about when football was the subject. But I was not too keen on his criticisms about specific people. I could not see why he took it upon himself to criticize other clubs and their players.

All right, he was being honest. I like to think I am an honest man. But absolute honesty declared is *not* always the best policy. If we were all comprehensively honest we would go round making enemies of almost everybody we met. It is perfectly honest if a man has a pimple on the end of his nose to tell him so. But he is more aware of it than anyone else in the world. He is not thrusting it at you. He would rather hide it from you. It is equally honest to say nothing about the pimple on a man's nose. It is equally honest to criticize without being too personal about it. I can see that I have fallen into my own trap. I have made a personal observation about Brian Clough's sing-song speech. I am criticizing his forthrightness. But my observation about the speech was only to suggest that he lost the impact of some of the better things he said by the sound of it when it came out.

Perhaps a little smile at the end of a sentence might help. But I suppose even a smile could be dishonest and he wouldn't want that.

I hope that my criticisms will be accepted. I doubt that

they will. Brian Clough was only thirty-six when Derby won that Championship, a prodigious performance. And the young are apt to be messianic. Fathers of sons – and daughters – will not need to be reminded that the young think the old fellow is talking through his square hat.

Brian Clough's achievements speak for themselves. A man who can go straight from the painful wreckage of a brilliant playing career and take on a humble club like Hartlepool United as manager, go begging for money to help them along, sweep dressing rooms and do other chores to save money for them and give them some basis for the future, is built of the stuff that football needs.

I admire his insistence on giving credit to the part played by the man he chooses to call his partner rather than his assistant, Peter Taylor, who was with him as a goalkeeper at Middlesbrough, and who joined him in the struggle at Hartlepool – a real partnership after my own heart, and another example of Clough's judgement in realizing that football cannot be a one-man job.

I am being perfectly honest when I say I hope that Brian Clough does not talk so much that he puts his foot in it. Sometimes, like Malcolm Allison in his noisier days, he sounds like Cassius Clay, sorry, Muhammed Ali. But Ali backs his forecasts himself. He doesn't depend on a team doing it for him. Brian Clough can handle players. That much he has proved. But once on the pitch they are on their own. Form plays strange tricks at the most unlikely times. Other teams' form as well as your own team's. Sometimes it is their day. Sometimes it is yours. It is unpredictable.

Meanwhile for the full test we shall have to see what Brian Clough does in time and what time does to Brian Clough. He is very young and therefore there is not much we can do about him.

JOCK STEIN

Around 1942, in my Army days, I was posted to Kelso, and I played as a guest for Hibernian. In one of our matches a young stripling played against us for Albion Rovers, a centre-half whose name meant nothing to me. It was Jock Stein. Nor did I see any more of him until much later. He went playing for Llanelly, a non-League club, from whom

141

he joined Celtic, and it was when he played for them that I next came across him, in action against Manchester United under my managership, in a Coronation Cup match. Celtic beat us.

Jock became Celtic's captain, then their coach, and then he went as manager to Dunfermline in 1960, saved them from relegation and led them to a Scottish Cup win by beating Celtic in the Final. It was merely the beginning of an astonishingly successful managerial career.

He joined Hibernian as manager in 1964, took them from the depths to up among the leaders, and after less than a year in that job went back to his old love Celtic, who had changed his life, and Scottish football's history, by having the judgement to bring him from Llanelly in 1951. Celtic thereafter towered over Scottish football, reaching the ultimate in the 1966-7 season by winning everything they tried for, the European Cup, the Scottish Cup, the League and the League Cup.

In doing all this Jock Stein never deviated from his idea that football should be an attacking, entertaining game. He succeeded by communication and by gaining respect and affection.

STAN CULLIS

Of all the opposition in my time none strove harder to whack the life out of me than Stan Cullis, a top centre-half who became a top manager. A strong, no-nonsense character, Stan. Yet an interesting sidelight on this tough fellow is that his happiest day was when his son decided to forego better paid professions to become a clergyman. And I know that after the Munich crash Stan's son and daughter prayed for me.

For all that, Cullis the professional, who as a player was kind enough to say that I was the only one he modelled his game on, did not, as a manager, allow the crash to stop him from beating United to win the 1957-8 championship.

Stan Cullis's Wolverhampton team were, like him, honest, unambiguous, uncomplicated, making full use of wingers like Jimmy Mullen and Johnny Hancocks and straightforward players like Billy Wright and Ron Flowers behind them.

Under Stan Wolves won three League championships and the FA Cup twice. He gave a lot to football, but as I write he is not in any big job in the game, and football is not so rich in human wealth that it can spare such a man.

BILL SHANKLY

The passion of Bill Shankly for football is legendary. His marriage to the game has been the greatest love-match in its history. He loved football as a boy, and possibly no more than many another boy. I doubt that he lived it any more than I did. But the love became an even deeper affection, a passion, when he was told that, instead of working down a mine digging for coal and fitting in his football when he could, somebody was anxious to *pay* him for playing the game he would have walked miles to play for nothing.

I believe he has never ceased to wonder about it. I believe he has spent the rest of his life since that wonderful day in repaying the game, with his skill and his indefatigable effort, for the joy it has given him. He simply cannot understand any player who can have less than complete devotion and ceaseless enthusiasm for it. As a young player, as an experienced international, as a young manager, as an experienced manager, his drive and enthusiasm never diminished. From the start he could not have been any more dedicated to his team and to the game itself. His passion did not diminish when his first successful Liverpool team felt the ravages of time and dispersed. It could not diminish.

Bill's very enthusiasm must have made the going harder because he could never countenance anything less than complete enthusiasm in others, and by Shankly standards few could be perfect in this regard. But I would not tell him that, because all Bill's players were always the greatest, and woe betide the person who disagreed about it. Furthermore, Bill's enthusiasm rubbed off on others, so there could never be a half-hearted Liverpool team in his time.

But I have no doubt he was disenchanted with situations from time to time. I recall once, in his earlier days at Liverpool, something had really rubbed him up the wrong way, so much so that he told me he was going to resign from the managership. I asked him had he a job to go to and he hadn't. Bill Shankly was always so infatuated with football that money was coincidental to the job and the game. Whatever the trouble was, he felt it strongly, and the fact that he would not have a job and therefore would not have any wages would scarcely have entered his head.

There was something he didn't like and he would go. It was as simple as that. I influenced him to stay. I said: 'Bill, things are bound to break for you.' In only a few weeks after that things *did* begin to break for him. And Liverpool became a power in the land.

His players were not, as Shanks would have had us all believe, the greatest in the world. But they ran their hearts out for him. They played as if they would have died for Liverpool. He told the world they were even greater than they were and they believed him and became greater than they were. This is real coaching. Regimenting is not coaching. Inspiring is coaching.

He would blast hell out of any man who made him angry and then it would be forgotten. Only little men bear grudges. His love for Liverpool and its loyal supporters and the noisy, singing, wisecracking Kop in particular, knew no bounds. But had he landed up at Hartlepool his love would not have been less.

His repertoire of wisecracks was boundless, too. They came spilling out, one for every occasion. And they got around. 'Have you heard the latest Shanks? He went into this barber's shop, see, and the barber said "Short back and sides as usual Mr Shankly and plenty off the top?" and Shanks said: "Aye, Everton!"' Or the tale of when he dropped a player and someone said 'Why did you drop so-and-so, Mr Shankly?' and Shanks said: 'Drop him? I should have dropped him down the pit weeks ago.'

Then there was the straightforward summing up. Like when Celtic won the European Cup Final against Inter-Milan and Shanks said to Celtic's manager, Jock Stein: 'You will be immortal! Mind you, *we'd* have beaten that lot.'

On his dedication as a player Bill Shankly once said: 'I was not satisfied unless I could *sprint* for ninety minutes let alone play for ninety minutes.' So it seems 'running' in football was not invented in the Sixties.

On fitness: 'You can get so fit that you are almost immune from injuries – like a rubber ball.'

The young fellow with a Fernandel face, a tall, toothy smile and a pair of legs like parentheses, was an Everton player and I by now a Liverpool player. His name was Joe Mercer and he wasn't very happy. He was frustrated. He couldn't get into the first team. It was one of those spells all players suffer from sometime in their career, but it was unlike Joe Mercer to be miserable. Even by then I had found myself to be one of those people who apparently have a ready shoulder to cry on, although not many Everton players cry on the shoulders of Liverpool players. 'I think I should be in the first team, Matt,' he said. 'I would like your advice.' So I said: 'The only thing to do is to force yourself into the first team. Get down to it, show them you have so much ability that they can't keep you out.' He did, and he became an England wing-half.

I came across him later in the Army in Greece and Italy, where as 'manager' of the Army team I put him in charge of rations, in which he was as good a provider of food as he was at telling passes. Next I met him when he was captain of England and I of Scotland, and there was never a craftier opponent. By the time he had moved from Everton to Arsenal I was manager of Manchester United. Only a broken leg ended his playing career at the venerable age of forty.

Joe now made the natural move into managership, in which capacity he left Sheffield United for Aston Villa, where he had a sickener and then became literally sick. It seemed he had done with football for good, but as Joe often told me: 'Football can do without me but I can't do without football.' In a move that was a big surprise to most people he made a come-back with Manchester City, at once becoming my sternest opponent and smiling neighbour in Chorlton-cum-Hardy, as well as remaining my old and very dear friend. There he set out to dispute the hitherto undisputed title of United as champions of Manchester.

As soon as he set foot into Maine Road Joe lifted the gloom that had enveloped Manchester City. He seemed to give stature and stability to the place immediately. The glow of his cheery face helped, but only because it was the happy façade that covered one of the real football brains.

He exuded authority. He had status. By this time he had discovered that he couldn't win Manchester, let alone the world, unassisted, and only a week after his appointment he signed up Malcolm Allison as his right-hand man.

The partnership of Mercer and Allison was a merger of craft and drive. Both men had that indefinable quality, personality, both were extrovert, both football experts, both were humorists, the elder, Mercer, the authoritative, talkative diplomat, the younger, Allison, the authoritative, talkative, undiplomatic zealot. They were different. They were complementary. Malcolm, notwithstanding an illness that cost him half a lung, had seemingly limitless energy. He drove himself and his players unmercifully but, with imaginative variety in training, and a persuasive as well as noisy tongue, he made players feel that if they would simply give more than they thought they could give, if they would hurt themselves with effort, they would, like Bill Shankly's Liverpool men, be the greatest.

When Allison's storms blew, Mercer becalmed them. Joe enhanced his own standing as one of the game's best-loved figures as well as one of the game's best brains. His popularity never diminished. Anybody – players, spectators, television viewers – could expect a straight answer that went to the very root of a situation without any sign of pedantry.

Malcolm sometimes seemed to go out of his way, with outrageous claims, outrageous forecasts, and excesses of enthusiasm that brought trouble only to himself, and an excess of loud noises, all without in any way reducing his brilliance as a coach, to make himself unpopular with people who did not understand that sometimes his noises were made with tongue in cheek. The Cassius Clay of coaches, or Muhammed Allison if he prefers it, could be heard the length and breadth of the land. Like Cassius he didn't speak from an empty head. Malcolm had something to offer.

Joe Mercer and Malcolm Allison changed a huge inferiority complex at Manchester City into a superiority complex. In their first season, 1965-6, at Maine Road, City won the Second Division Championship. In season 1967-8 they won the First Division Championship, in 1968-9 they won the FA Cup, and in 1970 they won the European Cup-winners' Cup.

Their supporters claimed the championship of Manchester for City in the Mercer-Allison era, during which time United merely won the First Division Championship in season 1966-7, were runners-up in 1967-8, were in the last of five FA Cup semi-finals in succession, won the European Cup in 1968 and were in the semi-final of the European Cup in 1969. That's all.

Moreover, United remained Manchester champions for attendances, which fact annoyed Malcolm Allison profoundly. He had always been extremely irritated to see such a preponderance of red scarves in Manchester. I think it was a 'thing' with him. This may well have provoked him to say once when City were lucky to get away with a draw against United: 'We should have won by six or seven.'

But, of course, this was all for the benefit of listeners and must surely have been a joke. In any case I am a great admirer of Allison's work, and I have had more than one enjoyable and serious conversation with him. He knows his act, or his acting, has never kidded me.

Tactically, the City style changed more than once even under Mercer and Allison. At first they were positive with a slight hint of caution. That made them set a certain player on to a certain player, which always smacks of inferiority complex to me but is perhaps forgivable when you are first blending a team. They then became confident and positive, and really their most attractive period was this middle bit. It came as a surprise to me when at the beginning of the 1972-3 season it appeared Allison was toying with the idea of playing that magnificent winger Mike Summerbee in a deeper position. I preferred my Allisons positive – and my Summerbees.

But before that time Joe Mercer was gone, not from the game altogether, but to Coventry City. I miss my games of golf with him. We are just about a match for each other at that. We solved all football's problems on the golf course, a comfortable place to solve them, but as everybody knows, golf-course conversations, even if they were fit to print, are off the record.

Malcolm Allison became manager, with no wise man directing the general strategy, or listening to him blow up, or just chatting about players and places, strengths and weaknesses, or players needed and players not needed. Football managership is a frightening job without these blood-brothers.

Almost immediately, Malcolm began to make fewer loud noises. The wider you open your mouth as a manager, the more liable you are to put your foot in it. Now he was entitled to take the praise for any success that came along. Be sure if it didn't he would be given the blame. Because he was now the man who made all the decisions.

Then suddenly, Manchester City lost their remaining half of the Mercer-Allison partnership. Malcolm moved to Crystal Palace as team-manager. He was a brilliant coach. He may well prove to be a brilliant manager. In ten years' time we shall know.

SIR ALF

With hindsight, it seems incredible that England international football teams, not to mention Ireland, Scotland and Wales teams, were ever selected by non-professional people who, with all the goodwill in the world and whatever experience they had in football's administrative affairs, were simply not so well qualified as professional football men to select them. It is like a club's directors picking the club team. Do I hear a whisper that some directors do still stick their noses in?

The fact that several selectors joined in the game of selecting does not mean that the system was several times as good. It was several times as bad as one non-professional selector having the last word. Moreover six *professional* selectors on one committee, each finding the players that suited him and then all trying to sort out a team from the bunch, would be six times as inefficient as one. A few tips from experts on how certain players are shaping at the moment, or a query whether they have seen any good prospects lately, are a great help. But only one man can pick a team.

Walter Winterbottom was given the joint task of being England's team manager and the FA's chief coach and he had to try to extricate England from the football mess it had got itself into as far as the rest of the world was concerned.

But not until it was decided that the England managership was quite big enough a job to occupy one man all his working hours was any real progress made.

One of the players in the England team humiliated by the Hungarians at Wembley in 1953 was Alf Ramsey, a studious right full-back who played first for Southampton and then Tottenham Hotspur.

His playing days over, Alf became manager of Ipswich Town, a humble Third Division club. Making the most of the almost anonymous players he had, he took Ipswich to promotion (1956-7) and then, in consecutive years (1960-1 and 1961-2), won the Second and then the First Division Championships, which was one of the only two football miracles in my time. (The other was the defeat of England in the 1950 World Cup by the United States! England's right-back that day was Alf Ramsey and the team was: Williams; Ramsey, Aston; Wright, Hughes, Dickinson; Finney, Mannion, Bentley, Mortensen, Mullen.)

In 1963 Alf Ramsey took over the England team managership. The idea was to try to build a team that would have some hope in the 1966 World Cup in England. There were not many signs of that during Alf's beginnings. Then I remember he called in a few managers, of whom I was one, with the idea of discussing any angles that might help him in his building. One of the things he said was that he could not find wingers to his satisfaction. He had seen the Argentinians and he thought it might pay him to try out their system, which was minus wingers, and came to be known as four-three-three (four at the back, three in the middle and three up front).

So were born England's Wingless Wonders. The system was that England had an extra one in the middle and an extra one back, with full-backs overlapping like wingers, but the main idea being to secure the middle and make use of the sudden break, the four at the back also being less vulnerable than three. It was a defensive measure, more cautious than confident, more negative than positive. The break could happen from any one – so the right sort of players were needed. Possibly Martin Peters was the best example of what Alf aimed at. He appeared with startling suddenness. Now he was one of the near anonymous mass in the middle. Now he was in a position, seemingly anywhere at all, ready to score.

Alf's first success with the method was in Madrid in 1965. I saw the match. England beat Spain 2-0. He had signs of a real team at last. It was great encouragement, something for England's players to get their teeth into. It wasn't pretty. But it worked. It gave Alf and his players confidence. Then the right results kept coming along and Alf's Wingless Wonders won the World Cup.

Whatever his critics have said, and I for one loathe and detest negative football, Sir Alf Ramsey has done a wonderful job. He is an extremely learned student of the game. He knows every angle of it. The method and the attention to detail reflected the man. After 1966 England had good results and bad ones. His greatest single mistake was in taking off Bobby Charlton (substituted by Colin Bell) in the World Cup match against West Germany in Mexico. England led 2-0 with twenty minutes to go. Then Beckenbauer scored and Bell was on for Charlton at the kick-off after the goal. Hunter also subbed for Martin Peters, but I believe the withdrawal of Charlton, which gave Beckenbauer more freedom for the rest of the match, was the chief reason why the Germans went on to equalize and then win 3-2 in extra time.

Trying to read Alf's mind I decided that his reason was probably to save Charlton for the semi-final that seemed certain for England. But, always a creative-type manager myself, I would have preferred a more positive approach generally by Alf. Conscious though I always was that the defence must be strong, I liked my teams to 'go at them', rather than put safety first and depend on the break.

West Germany outclassed England in 1972 and Alf had his critics again. Perhaps good breakers had now become scarce. This job needs a very sharp and able character and a perceptive mind. It is not a job for what are known as ball-winners who, by and large, are lost when it comes to creating anything. Thus the game foundered on a lack of wingers *and* a lack of breakers. The Germans at any rate showed that the positive can beat the negative, that a team can play attractively, entertainingly and win, that fear and caution is unnecessary with creative players, that, in a few words, the old four-three-three (or even worse, the four-four-two) had had its day, at any rate as far as world-class football was concerned.

No method lasts for ever in football. The counter will surely come. It is hard to begin again when a system has worked and won the World Cup. A new method might fail. But it surely had to be tried. Unhappily the 1966 World Cup win, which gave one of the big thrills of their lives to British football supporters and to millions who had never been to a football match, also had the effect of so impressing the professional coaches that they 'joined the club'.

I suppose since Alf had said he couldn't find suitable wingers the clubs could say they had none to provide him with and that therefore his method would be good for them. The real reason, I feel, was that managers of teams with little individual talent saw it as a life-saver for them, and, in fear for their jobs (who can blame them for that!), grabbed the chance to organize their charges into teams who set out not to lose. It was a life-saver for coaches, too, since it gave them a chance to organize. Therefore as England had become an unentertaining team even in success, a negative team, English football became a less and less entertaining, more negative game as more and more clubs tried the method.

So Alf Ramsey, who created the monster, now had to kill it before it killed him. I do not imply that his job was in danger. I do imply that failure would be a terrible affront to the pride he was entitled to have. I believe he will change it. And however he changes it the players will be with him. Because Alf recognized from the start what I have always regarded as the golden rule of managership. He gained the respect of his players. And he gained their affection.

Ask any player who ever played for an England team under Alf Ramsey and he will eulogize 'Alf'. It cannot be coincidence that players of vastly different temperaments are as one in this matter. This, indeed, is the greatest quality of his managership. He gained their respect and affection both as a technical manager and as a person, as a boss. On the other hand, critics – and I do not mean only Press critics – have felt that he was inflexible, and I am inclined to the view that this sometimes was true. I am not at all certain that coaches and managers who thought he should use them as a team of technical helpers or even as a team of trainer-coaches or as a team of advisers were right. When it comes to decisions a manager has to be a dictator. Advice is all right when it is asked for, and I have asked for plenty of it in my time. But when it comes to decisions there can be only one boss.

Alf was not the easiest man in the world when it came to getting inside him, getting his real thoughts to come out. I found him quite prepared to discuss football. He phoned me several times and he welcomed advice, and then he decided for himself and quite rightly. But he was a bit touchy about any criticism of his team's performance or of his team itself. He was reluctant to admit failure by his players when they indeed failed. Judged by the way the players got on with him, his aloofness would seem to have been superficial, a façade, possibly a defence against a hundred and one self-declared experts. But aloof he seemed to be nevertheless.

Alf had a strong mind. He weighed up a situation, made his own decisions, and stuck to them. There was a paradox in some of his selections, or at least there seemed to be. Alf himself was a cultured player. I have to say that some of his choices would scarcely come into that category, some of them, possibly, being picked for their work-rate rather than their ability. But he was not the first cultured player to select his own opposites. Some tough players when they became managers have sought the gentler, prettier, more able players than they were themselves. Perhaps they picked the sort of players they would like to have been.

It would seem that Alf saw a system that might suit him and then chose players to suit that system. It is intriguing to cogitate on what Alf would have done with Stan Matthews in his four-three-three set-up. True, Alf has said he couldn't find wingers to suit him. But would he have changed the plan to suit Matthews? I have read of Alf telling players to go out and play their club game. Well, since almost every club began to play exactly the same four-three-three game, this scarcely taxed their ingenuity. It might well be that there was a shortage of geniuses, of players who could make England as attractive, say, as Brazil or West Germany.

It is hard to pass an opinion on this. The only real way to

find out is for managers to formulate a plan to suit the players, allowing an individual's talents to be tried and tested, instead of finding players to fit into a preconceived plan.

If clubs did not do this, Alf had not a hope of finding a team of real talents. How can a good winger be identified if he spends most of his time in the middle of the park in an anonymous bunch? I have said that the great, the genius will out. There were never more than a handful of them. But some possibly near-geniuses could scarcely emerge because fear crowded them into positions devised for men with half their talent, alongside players who had scarcely any.

It may be that there are not the geniuses today, the entertainers, but it does not seem logical that the usual select quota of them is not among us. I remember Alf bringing on Mike Summerbee as a substitute in one match and suddenly the game became exciting because he immediately began creating havoc on the right wing. It seemed to me that in Summerbee, for example, Alf *had* a winger who could make real use of a wing, with power, speed, and skill the like of which few overlapping full-backs could match, unless, like Terry Cooper of Leeds, they had already been wingers. I don't say Summerbee was a genius, but anybody better would have to be. Yet even Manchester City were known to play him in deeper positions.

Alf Ramsey did all the proving he needed to do about his managership. I hope his search for geniuses is successful, so that he can change the game again and succeed again when he has changed it. I believe only international-class craftsmen should be in the England team – in any position. Only from international-class players shall we get appropriately entertaining football. Then when Alf has given the example to follow, the coaches of the clubs will follow it. After all, if the modern fashion of strictly mechanical method football were played to perfection it would be a bore and even more predictable than it is now. And still clubs would finish bottom and be relegated and still managers would be fired for it.

It may sound like anarchy, but I would like to see a team of great individual players given their head in an international match. Great individual players have the knack of being good for each other. With Alf Ramsey at their head to provide the little order that might be needed for their seeming indiscipline and for their non-conforming to dull practices that have plagued the modern game, some permutation of England's best twenty or so ball-players would respond to him as all his players have done in the past. Then we could match West Germany or Brazil skill for skill.

But if we start off by saying that we haven't any great players, or there is an unusual shortage of them, we might just as well opt out now. Donkeys have their uses, but not among thoroughbreds. Alf would have a better chance of spotting the thoroughbreds if the League game became brave again and not stricken with fear. Alf himself was cautious, but never afraid.

Meanwhile I wish him luck. The man who restored our lost football pride deserves it.

PART FIVE

BEHIND THE SCENES

SIR STANLEY ROUS: FOOTBALL STATESMAN

The greatest man I have met in football is Sir Stanley Rous.

I say this unequivocally because not only has he influenced the game for its own good more than any other man, first in England and then all over the world, but also because he has done so with unwavering dignity.

My first sight of him was in the dressing room at Wembley in 1934. I was a member of the Manchester City team waiting to go out for the FA Cup Final against Portsmouth. We had lost the year before to Everton, and only losing Finalists can appreciate the feeling that engenders. So if anything we were perhaps even a bit jumpier than most Finalists, though we may not have shown it.

Some fifteen or twenty minutes before the kick-off was due, a tall, distinguished-looking man in referee's kit marched in and announced himself as Stanley Rous. I cannot remember that he had ever officiated in one of my matches before, though he had been in charge of many games in far corners of the world even then.

He told us he hoped the game would be a party piece, that the eyes of royalty, aye, the eyes of the world were on us. He wanted a keen, competitive match played strictly to the rules. We won 2–1. And after the match, S. F. Rous, as he was known as then, came to me and, to my great surprise and gratification, complimented me on the team's victory and my personal contribution to it. Perhaps he said the same to other players. I do not know. Certainly I appreciated the gesture.

At the celebration banquet the same evening a cheque was presented to Sir Frederick Wall, for his long service as secretary of the Football Association. Little did I know then that soon to be Sir Frederick's successor, that same year indeed, was the man who had refereed our Cup Final that day. And what a wonderful successor S. F. Rous turned out to be!

This school gamesmaster, an all-round sportsman himself, took on an enormous task, but a task well within his vast capacity for organization, a task that gave him scope for his efficiency, an efficiency that never narrowed his vision, which took in the whole panorama of British football as related to world football years before the British home countries caught on.

We had left FIFA (the Federation of International Football Associations) in 1928. And British football, in its cocoon, went on its way with unjustified claims to the Kingdom of the Football World as if by right because we invented it, blindly unaware that football's boundaries were ever broadening, blissfully (or slothfully) unconscious that other countries had caught us and passed us.

For years Stanley Rous warned us. He warned of Continental progress. He warned of their superior coaching techniques. He preached fearlessly, but never without dignity, and almost always he was proved right.

He was a bit too far-seeing for some, and there was at least one time when he had to climb down in the face of critics in the game. But he could see things when they wouldn't see things.

In 1946 we rejoined FIFA. But we did not really learn how sadly our football had lagged behind until the Hungarians came and humiliated England at Wembley in 1953. They were so far ahead of England in techniques, indeed, that it looked as if the teams were playing a different game.

It was no more than Sir Stanley had for long foreseen.

Sir Stanley had my ideas about management. In 1948, when his protégé, Walter Winterbottom, the England team manager and FA director of coaching, was away on England duty, I was asked to manage the British Olympic Soccer team.

Sir Stanley, in the chair at a meeting of representatives of the home associations, said in his opening remarks: 'Gentlemen, we have all appointed Matt Busby as manager of the British team. I want him to be manager in the fullest possible sense – responsible for the team and the players, with no interference by any of us.'

We managed to reach the semi-final, by luck and/or my

management, but whatever it was it was a considerable performance by a British team almost absolutely in the dark about the quality of football outside.

Sir Stanley Rous (knighted in 1949) carried on with his mission, the mission to raise our standards, to catch up with the world outside. His emergence as a world figure was inevitable. His presence, his knowledge, his vision, his principles that inspired him to say things fearlessly, sometimes risking his own popularity in doing so, his sense of fair play and his dignity made it so. Wherever he went, whatever he said, people listened. And as surely as night follows day, when FIFA, the world ruling body, were ready to elect a new President in 1961, Sir Stanley Rous was that man.

No man loves his country more than Stanley Rous. Yet he is big enough to subdue his patriotism in the certain knowledge that if football on a world scale is worth anything at all, it is as a sport, in which case nationalism, at least in its top administrators, must be subjugated. If sport and fair play are not synonymous they are neither sport nor fair play. Ideally, sport at any level should be conducted and watched without partisanship, but since football is a physical game of stress as well as skill, and even watching it sets the adrenalin moving and the emotions alternating between heights and depths, that ideal is unattainable.

It is the men at the top, and the top is FIFA, who must be fair to all nations and be seen to be fair. The man with the whole of the world of football in his hands is holding emotional dynamite. Stanley Rous is the ideal top man. And it is a tribute to him that, although he never shrinks from expressing opinions, he has never lost one ounce of dignity or respect. All nations, all races, look up to him. We have had no better ambassador.

Sir Stanley Rous is a great man. He is an approachable man. But, of course, great men always are.

THE MAN IN BLACK

Football is our finest safety valve. I do not claim that as an original thought. In 1959 Lord Westwood, who later became chairman of Newcastle United, quoted it as an opinion of his late father, the first Baron Westwood, who not only believed that this was so, but also set out a week in the life of a football supporter as evidence. Saturday: The match. Sunday: Re-living the match in a club, a pub and at home. Monday: Re-living the match at work. Tuesday: Wondering and arguing about what the team for the next match would be. Wednesday: Discussing the team picked and arguing what team should have been picked. Thursday: Football coupon. Friday: Pay day and talk about tomorrow's match. Saturday: Start again.

To this the late Lord Westwood could have added and doubtless the present Lord Westwood, with his sense of fun (he must be the most entertaining public speaker in football), *would* add, that football provides a chance for a man who is otherwise inhibited by his wife or his work to let off steam and shout to his heart's content.

The fact is that no two people see a football match in exactly the same way. Football people, including players, managers, coaches, directors, tea-ladies, and supporters, to name but three-quarters of a million who go to watch it and several million who watch it at home, buckshee, on the box, all have opinions about it. Some people who don't have opinions about anything else seem to have opinions about football, from boys of six to grannies of eighty-six. And a good thing it is for football, too, that argument on the game is so rife. What a dull game it would be if we all agreed about it! Certainly no one would go to watch it if we did.

In view of this, how can a man possibly be so masochistic or so egoistic as to become a referee?

We can in our millions argue until we are blue in the face but in deciding matters of fact in a match only one opinion counts, the opinion of the referee. 'What a lunatic decision!' 'Diabolical decision!' Who has not said something impolite about a referee's opinion on a matter of fact? Yet the referee is neither a lunatic nor a devil. He is simply a man with an opinion, the same as the rest of us. But in expressing ours we are wasting our time as far as the incident itself is concerned. The referee's decision is irrevocable unless he revokes it immediately himself, perhaps after consulting a linesman. And quite rightly so. Football wouldn't work if it were not.

Unfortunately, in anything but the most obvious decision

the referee will be wrong in the opinion of many, and he is almost never deemed unanimously to be right. Even referees themselves differ in interpretations of laws, and they are all experts on the wording of them and could doubtless recite them verbatim. In a game in which, for instance, under the laws *intent* is a prerequisite for a happening to be an offence, the referee has necessarily to be allowed his discretion, and discretion is by human nature flexible and perhaps even inconsistent in one man, according to situations and his moods, so inconsistencies in matters of the discretion of *many* referees are inevitable no matter how big the effort to remove those inconsistencies.

To add to the referee's problems, he has to make virtually *instant* decisions, which increase the margin of error. Anybody who has watched football, even for half a century, finds it difficult to make decisions even to himself about half the things that happen in a match. I recommend doubters to try it. It is one thing seeing an incident and chatting to your neighbours about it and sorting the whole thing and deciding the referee was an idiot to give such a decision. It is another to decide at the moment it happens, without debate with anyone else. The referee has no television play-backs. The playback may well show the referee to have been incorrect in a decision, or *appear* to do so. But it is grossly unfair to use a playback as evidence against a referee, however fair it is to use it as evidence in defence of a player in front of a disciplinary commission.

Because no man can be expected to be infallible. He must be allowed his quota of mistakes. When American Edward J. Phelps said in a speech in the Mansion House, London, in 1889: 'The man who makes no mistakes does not usually make anything', he sure said a mouthful, if I may borrow from his homeland. The Football League was born one year before he said it and though I do not suppose that he was making an appeal for fair play to referees I am sorry that so few referees' critics have heeded him.

So, since nobody loves referees except referees' mums, and since referees are never unanimously right, and since they are the only persons in a match whose opinions count, what manner of man will take on the job? In the nicest possible way I say it, because I would not have had my good life had it not been for referees, without whom there would have

160

not been any football to provide it for me, and I repeat I mean it in the nicest possible way, a man has to be something of an egoist to do a job which requires him to make a decision (in other words pass an opinion) that a large number of people will disagree with and say: 'That's what I have decided. Think what you like.' In the nicest possible way I say that to dress up in a natty little black outfit of black top and black shorts and shiny football boots that almost never foot a ball, before a crowd of thousands of people who are ready to jeer you, never cheer you, ready to laugh at you if you slip on your backside, and at *best* to ignore you, a man has to be something of a showman, as all players are and therefore as I suppose I must also have been.

A man who takes on this sort of job must also have great confidence in his ability to handle men, twenty-two men plus substitutes, each with his own personality which is different from all the others. In other words he must like being a boss. Otherwise their very fame must overwhelm him. Moreover he must be brave. A coward need not apply for a job in which once or twice per week he may well find thousands of people screaming at him, a frightening experience indeed, so he must be a man confident in his backbone, be thick-skinned, and be resilient to boot. He must feel he is fit enough to keep up with a game in which players spend almost all week getting fit.

He must love the game.

Luckily such men keep coming up. There are firm ones, and 'easy' ones, thin ones and fat ones. There are long ones and short ones, jolly ones and glum ones. There are extroverts and introverts, quiet ones and loud ones. There are thatched ones and bald ones, shy ones and showy ones. Their ambition and reward, unless they are the pick of the bunch and even if they are the pick of the bunch, is the FA Cup Final at Wembley. In a match, the best they can hope for is not to be noticed at all, than which surely for any job in life there can be no more negative reward. In a press report the best they can hope for is not to be mentioned.

The best of our referees would be hard to beat anywhere. They are in demand all over the world, for the biggest competitions. The greatest of them have been abused. The greatest have made mistakes.

After a game the referee is at the mercy of the clubs. The winners probably hold him in high esteem, and give him marks to show it. Losers may hold him in less esteem and mark accordingly. Yet for all the abuse heaped upon even the best of these men, they come back for more, again and again. Few of them volunteer to retire. They are a people apart.

The best of them, like the best of footballers, the best of motor mechanics, the best of butchers and electric light makers, are gifted. Techniques are improved with experience. Personality changes not. The diffident starter at thirty who becomes the fuss-pot at thirty-five was always a fuss-pot under the skin. The intangible gift that counts for most is presence. A man with the gift of presence attracts attention to himself without trying. You can see him in a crowd, whatever size or shape he is. A referee with the gift of presence – epitomized by Stanley Rous – doesn't have to tell players he is not going to put up with any nonsense. One look at him and they would not dream of committing any nonsense. At most a quiet word from him is enough.

A referee has to be firm. Players do not like him any the less if he is. He might be cheerful. He might be sombre. But he must not be weak. The players sort referees out as they sort opponents out. If the referee is 'easy' the sillier ones among them will take advantage. Sillier, I say, because however frustrated a player might become when he thinks the referee has made a mistake he cannot beat the referee. On the other hand if the referee has a reputation for pouncing on anything, serious or trivial, the buzz goes round the dressing room. 'Watch out. This fellow won't stand any nonsense.'

For all their exertions, referees receive only £10.50 per match plus expenses. It should be more. They are professionals already, since they are paid. But let us make it a worthwhile profession.

LAW AND ORDER

Obviously a referee needs to have a coherent set of laws behind him, and the means of enforcing them. That football has altered its laws so little in its long history is a tribute to its founders rather than a criticism of its subsequent administrators.

Nevertheless, there is something wrong with a law that can make a player offside a yard inside his opponent's half, and this is not the only weakness in a law that causes more trouble than any other. Nor did I ever like the possibility of a man's being played onside by an opponent's mere touch of the ball. I think a man should be offside or not. One or the other. Changes in this law are bound to come, just as they did in the matter of substitutes, which I advocated for a long time before they were legalized.

It is perhaps time now to examine the disciplinary procedures. But first an examination of illegal or violent play might be opportune. I had no trouble with referees, but I like to think I had as much heart as the next man and tackled opponents as determinedly. Unquestionably a player who goes halfheartedly into a tackle will not only fail to win the ball, but will make himself vulnerable to injury. If a fair and determined tackle is met fairly and determinedly seldom is either player injured. Determined is a clumsier word, perhaps, but that is what is meant when football people talk about 'hard' tackle.

There are bound to be some unfair tackles, many of which, however, are perpetrated by players who have not mastered the art of tackling. They do not time the tackle properly and therefore they arrive late with it, the ball is gone and the leg of the opponent is tackled instead. There are other players who do not know their own strength or do not appear to know it, seeming not to realize that a determined tackle by them has a clobbering effect on a slighter man. There are excitable players who let their enthusiasm get the better of them. There are players, happily not many of them, who are unscrupulous, who, for example will go 'over the ball' as a last resource, contacting the opponent's legs. There is no excuse for any tackle that sets out to get the ball at the calculated risk of injuring an opponent.

It could be that one reason why there seem to be more violent tackles now is that the fair shoulder charge seems virtually to have been banished. This is sad, because fair shoulder charging used to be part of the entertainment and seldom caused more injury than the wounded pride of the charged one, who added to the exhilaration by getting his own back with a charge later on. On the other hand I hate to think what some of the play-acting characters – those who are one second seen writhing in agony after a tackle and the next second running fifty yards in even time – would do if a good, healthy, bone-shaking shoulder charge should hit them.

All right, Manchester United under Matt Busby, who had no trouble himself with referees, and Leeds United under Don Revie, who had no trouble himself with referees, and many others like us, have had our share of players disciplined. But let us see what can be done about reducing violent play.

With many others, I felt that the points system was a step in the right direction. Suspension after twelve points seemed a likely deterrent. I thought it might help remove the dangerous and unfair tackling, and other of the game's ailments. In doing so it would give the talented player some protection from ruthless treatment. It seemed like a warning to players and clubs about the dangers of breaking the laws. And for a little while it did seem that much of the crude tackling of a player from behind was being eliminated. But the whole idea was damaged considerably by the excessive exercising of players' rights to appeal against cautions or bookings as they are popularly called.

Some appeals were obviously justified. But there were many appeals, justified and unjustified, successful and unsuccessful, which seemed even to contain an element of cheating because an appeal might postpone the disciplinary hearing and therefore ensure that a player could play, say, in an imminent match when the possibility of suspension loomed. The mass of appeals brought tremendous pressures, immense demands on the energy and time of Vernon Stokes and the men of his commissions.

Looking for an alternative, I felt that clubs and players should be made to suffer on the field as well as off it by inflicting instant punishment. Crimes would still have to be classified, but my hoped for remedy would be for a player, instead of being booked for a crime of violence, to be banished from the pitch instead for fifteen or twenty minutes.

Further misdemeanours would cause the player to be sent off for the rest of the match as before. If the crime warranted it, he would be sent off for the whole of the match in the first place, and subsequently 'tried' in the normal way. This reform would make clubs, managers, coaches and players aware of the perils of playing illegally. A team could be without an offending player for fifteen to twenty minutes and could lose a game because of it. A team could be without two or even three players if there were to be as many sin-bin banishments as there were the bookings they replaced.

Since, except for an offender who offended twice, there would be no further punishment for the crime, the great load on disciplinary commissions would be lessened.

I do not claim that the whole idea of the sin-bin is original. I recommended it in an article years ago. Others have suggested it. But I would like to see the face of a manager forced to watch his team minus two players, who might themselves enjoy the chance of a rest, but would not enjoy the fruits of their delinquency when the boss had examined the defeat it may well have caused.

It might be asked how a referee would decide whether a foul tackle was serious enough to warrant the sin-bin. My answer is that referees are not often wrong in detecting real violence.

The sin-bin could bring some of the goals so sadly lacking, because the clogger would be in peril, from his own manager, his colleagues, and everybody concerned with his club, and the genius would not be chopped down by the mediocre bully.

Another malady that distressed me was the situation when players chased or surrounded a referee, showing dissent, or arguing or going on like a nagging woman whenever a decision was given against them. Nothing could be more undignified. It offended the dignity of the referee and the players themselves looked like peevish schoolgirls. Constant repetition of this referee-badgering sometimes amounted to intimidation. The idea that only the captain, wearing a distinguishing armband, should be permitted even to speak to a referee about a decision, seemed to me to be a sensible one.

There is little wrong with the laws of the game. It is up to football to supplement them and bring offenders to heel. Here I must mention those offenders off the pitch who are the enemies of referees, players, and the game itself. One of the worst aspects of football in the Seventies is the behaviour and the language of some of the young people who watch it. I wish I could solve that problem. But if I could I would be a national benefactor. Because bad behaviour by young people at football matches is no more than a reflection of standards in our society in general. It is possible that if there were no football matches for gangs of young nuisances to go to they would be even bigger nuisances elsewhere. At least in a football ground they are penned in and not running loose in the streets, though they do sometimes do some damage in the streets before or after a game.

Perhaps there should be sin-bins for ruffian spectators as well as for ruffian footballers. Embarrassment, being made to look foolish in front of their friends, is one solution. Not long ago a young fan daubed some slogan or other on an hotel wall and was about to board the coach that was to take him home when a policeman grabbed him, took him into the hotel, asked for scrubbing brushes and hot water and told him he could join his friends in the coach when he had cleaned every speck of graffiti off the wall. This took about half an hour, and his pals gave him more verbal stick than they had given the referee.

It is certainly wrong to tar all the young people with the same brush. Indeed it is mainly the early-teens age group that chant the filth and break bones and windows. So much so that youths of about nineteen look down upon their cheeky juniors as if they had not grown up, which of course, they haven't. It is not surprising that some schoolteachers are physically afraid of the young hoodlums, and if society allows teachers to be intimidated by pupils, society must take the blame for the young people's extra-curricular goings-on and not lay the blame on football clubs who do their utmost to control the pests.

COACHING AND THE MODERN GAME

On 28 June 1971, I was invited as a member of the Technical Committee of UEFA (the Union of European Football Associations) to deliver a lecture to the chief coaches of Europe at Klosters, Switzerland. This is what I said:

Football has been changing ever since it started. But thanks to you gentlemen it has changed more in the last ten years than in the previous ninety.

You have applied science to a sport that had merely ambled along enjoying itself for itself and, indeed, Britain, the place it was born in, was so secure in its proprietorship of football, that scientifically it looked like being left behind.

'It's our game, so how can anybody else beat us at it?' seemed to be the idea.

Then we woke up. Or more like it, we were rudely awakened, most rudely of all by the Hungarians, and we were to find we were not in the same street as Brazil among others.

The Hungarians showed there was much more to football than just being good players. The Hungarians were good players. Some of them were great players. But they also used new methods, new positional arrangements, and baffled us.

We (I say 'we' as a Briton and not as a Scot) eventually caught up and England actually found a way, by coaching and using still different methods, to win the World Cup in 1966, the Brazilians having won it the previous twice.

I do not believe that England were the best individual footballers in 1966. But they turned out to be the best TEAM. I do not think England were the most entertaining footballers to watch. But they were winning footballers.

Then, next time, the Brazilians won it again. I believe they WERE the best footballers and they also turned out to be the best team. I believe they WERE the most entertaining footballers to watch. And they WERE winning footballers.

Their efficiency did not wipe the smile off their football.

It was a triumph for football ability, individual and collective ability. Even though the Brazilians trained scientifically I think their success was due more to brilliant individuals than to organization, though organized they certainly were.

I believe also their inherent ability flowers more abundantly than the Europeans' only because, as in Britain in

167

football's earlier days, many many Brazilian boys play football all day long almost from birth because they have little else to do, whereas the more affluent European boy often has other things to distract him, like the television, a ride in father's car, or studying for his examinations.

In other words footballers are produced in inverse ratio to increasing prosperity.

So the need for coaches in Europe is greater than in Brazil, and it will be interesting to see indeed if Brazil's footballer production diminishes with greater prosperity.

Meanwhile I am not unhappy to see the best footballers win the prizes, with due respect to you, gentlemen. Because I still like to see the brilliant individual in action.

It is in fact, for these reasons, up to you to apply yourselves, as you have been doing so diligently, to confounding me and coaching your teams to beat them.

But since competition gets keener and keener there are warning signs to you. I believe, in looking ahead. The great danger in coaching is that it might take all the fun out of football.

In the distant past, in fact in the not-too-distant past, the great player dominated to a far greater extent than he does today. The great player has always been outnumbered by ordinary players, but before we began to apply science and strategy to our tactics, before we began to think so deeply about things, the ordinary player was no more than an extra to the star of the film.

Great players are individuals. That's what makes them great players. They do not conform readily. They do the unexpected. That is also why they are great players. If they did what was expected they would be ordinary players.

It so happens that great players are also great passers of the ball. So the individual genius aids teamwork because HE gives ordinary players a ball that makes life easier for them.

But coaching changed things. Coaching is for ordinary players. It makes them better players. That maybe is why most great coaches were themselves ordinary players. They know how to improve an ordinary player's game because they had scope for improving themselves when they were players and did so improve themselves. Great players don't understand why lesser men can't do great things. They have

168

difficulty in explaining to others what they themselves do by instinct.

Far greater standards of fitness became required by coaches, so that what the ordinary player lacked in ability he compensated for to some extent by being fit to run a marathon and take the knocks at the same time. Incidentally I am not sure the public realize what stamina is needed these days to take a player through ninety minutes at the present pace in these ever increasingly competitive times.

No longer could a full-back afford to wait for his opposing winger to come along before he took part in the proceedings. No longer could a winger loiter on a wing until the ball came nicely to his feet.

Wingers and full-backs had constantly to be working instead, earning their corn, instead of leaving all the hard work to the poor old wing half-backs and inside-forwards, who in the old days had to work double time without double pay.

Everybody indeed was coached into running all the time, so that if a colleague was beaten another would be there to tackle his antagonist.

More than this, it became policy to pay special attention to the genius in the opposition. Until nowadays he has to be a genius indeed to survive a match without a scratch. The theory is, and it is a very effective one, that two ordinary players, or three at a pinch, can counter one genius.

This is all very well. But we have to be careful we do not drive individuality out of the game altogether.

This two-ordinary-players-on-to-one-genius idea is in fact a policy of negation. It is based on the premise that the first rule is to stop the other team instead of being to get on with the job of winning straight from the kick-off. And if football is to be a game of not-losing instead of a game of winning there is something radically wrong with it.

I believe that coaches, now that they have made a science of negation, are challenged to make a science of production. We cannot expect all teams to be like Brazil, brimful of ability.

The fact is that football is in great danger of becoming to enable coaches to apply themselves to the job of attacking too grim. A smiling player is a rare exception.

Greater rewards for goals would appear to be a necessity

instead of so much concentration on destroying opponents' attacks. I am afraid the points system has not kept pace with the coaching.

Goalscoring is what the game of football is all about, or what it should be all about. The creative move, whether by good passes, or by one man beating one or several opponents, the shot or header into the net, or the shot or header missed by inches, or a great save – these are the things that attract and excite and therefore *keep* spectators. Another is the individual brilliance that sometimes makes everything else look drab in comparison and often makes a goal possible.

There have been many suggestions, such as a kick-in instead of a throw-in, offside confined to an eighteen yard area, and so on. But I believe that some system of points for goals scored would be the greatest help in encouraging attacking and more entertaining football.

And entertain we must. Otherwise attendances will continue to go down and football as we know it will not survive.

We are all aware of the monster of the box – the television box I mean of course – and that many people may see enough football on it to last them a week. We are aware of the social trends, the motor car, the wife who wants her husband to take her shopping instead of *allowing* him to go to the match.

But football has to hit back for itself. It has to sell itself despite the competition. And I don't mean that it has to rely entirely on professional sellers or consultants, or those people who could sell vacuum cleaners or television sets to housewives.

Because it doesn't matter how good a salesman a man is, if his vacuum cleaner doesn't pick up the dust or his television set hasn't got much of a picture he won't sell so many, and those he sells will lose the goodwill of those he has sold them to.

No, we have to sell football that people will decide is worth buying. We have to make it an irresistible purchase. We have to attract people and we have to keep them. And to do so we have to excite them, to entertain them.

I don't care how efficient a team would seem to be by winning championships or cups by winning home games by a narrow margin and not losing away games. If they win

trophies by negative football they will not excite and entertain crowds.

There is an enormous number of people who are not
actually blinded by emotion towards their own favourite
team. They are like the 'don't knows' in the opinion polls.
There are enough of them sometimes to turn the result of
an election from one party to another. There are enough of
them to make small crowds into large ones. We must not
only keep our loyal supporters. We must sway the 'don't
knows' our way.

A spate of back passes to a goalkeeper, a long, dreary
series of passes sideways, backwards and almost never forward, unadventurous tactics like keeping possession at all
costs, mass withdrawal straight from the kick-off – these
things bore a crowd, even irritate them.

We have had more than enough of this. And so, I believe,
have the spectators. Goals must be the goal.

Given the chance and given the assistance of some points-
for-goals system I believe that you, gentlemen, are as well
capable of teaching creation as destruction, of teaching
attack as efficiently as defence. I believe you can make the
ordinary player, who after all is a very good player or he
wouldn't be in top-class football anyway, I believe you can
make him as good an attacker as you have made him a
defender, now running more forward than backward, now
making the play go forward and less desperately backward. All right, I know if one team is going forward the
other is going backward. But going forward should be the
aim.

I believe you would very much like to be more creative,
more attack-conscious in your thinking. I believe you
would dearly love to give your brilliant individualists more
scope for their talents. I believe you would dearly love your
own individually brilliant players to be given a chance to
entertain.

I believe you would rather have your well-organized
ordinary player helping your brilliant individuals in attack
than being too much concerned in the negative job of
double-marking the opposition's genius.

I do not want the stars mollycoddled. I simply want
opponents to be a little busier looking for goals for themselves than stopping the other team from scoring them.

I am certain you will find ways to preserve the efficiency
you have instilled in players by your own application, study,
and hard work, and yet be able to foster the individual
genius and therefore entertain the spectator. I am confident
you will be successful in your search for goals.

Indeed, given help in greater reward for scoring goals,
I know you can achieve these things. You had better. For
the game's sake.

We MUST bring a smile back on football's face.

I have no reason to revise the ideas in my Klosters speech.
I had nursed them too long before my lecture in 1971. Indeed, the cure for the disease of negative football became
ever more urgent. It all but killed the game in Italy before
threatening to do so in England. And since it gained such
a stranglehold I make no apology for saying that advance-
ment in coaching techniques reduced rather than enhanced
football's entertainment value. If football had died, coaches
would certainly have been accessories.

HOPES AND FEARS

Football has given me a wonderful life. It would not be true
to say that if I could go back in time I would have it all
happen again. The Munich crash caused too many hearts
to be broken for that. But the warmth of people towards
me wherever I have travelled, inside and outside football,
has been constant proof to me of the game's potential in
fostering international friendship.

This may seem nonsense when we read of brawls here
and football riots there. I have only to remind myself of
Estudiantes. But the brawls and the riots are mere blots on
the splendid football landscape, and not the fault of football.

Manchester United have had many tough games in Spain,
Portugal, Italy – almost everywhere in the football world.
Emotions have been high on the night, and the arguments
fierce. Yet everywhere I go people stop me in the street and
wish me well. I doubt that I have ever been provoked into
an argument on non-match days in a country that was my
host of the moment. Waiters, taxi-drivers, hotel customers,

men on building sites, rich men and poor men ask feelingly about me, about Manchester United, about Britain.

This friendliness can be fostered by friendliness and warmth in response and can be multiplied a thousandfold by any people who are prepared to understand that every day is not a match day.

I believe people are very conscious of the conduct of their national teams, and want to be proud of them. I know that all good players and all good supporters want to win. I do not believe that people want their teams to win *at all costs*. It is the foreign players who do not stoop to thuggery who are the popular visitors here, just as it is the sporting British players who are popular when they go abroad, whether to play, or on holiday, or on business.

The World Cup provides the ideal opportunity to bring this truth out for people of all nations to see – that people want more than exciting, adventurous football with the touch of genius from the great ones. They want to see it clean. They do not want to be ashamed of their own representatives, no matter how keen they are to see them win.

I write without knowledge of the qualifiers for the 1974 World Cup finals in Munich. I don't know whether England or Scotland or both will qualify. But whether it is Brazil, West Germany, East Germany, England, Scotland, Holland, Spain, Italy, Portugal, Argentine, Chile, Russia or any other who win it, I hope it goes to a team who scorn cheating and thuggery.

If anything *is* to be gained from football in the sense of promoting friendship between nations – and if friendship cannot be promoted through sport how *can* it be promoted? – it is to be gained by winning or losing with dignity. If there are nations whose people so lose themselves in their emotions as to encourage the thug and the cheat they can be educated only by example. And there is no better example to a thug than to be beaten by a clean fighter. The defeat embarrasses the thug's supporters as much as it does the thug.

I hope sincerely that a defensive-minded team does not win the World Cup, be it England, Scotland, Brazil or any other. I was glad the Brazilians won the last one because they were attackers from forward to full-back and they were the best footballers. The Germans must have a chance

173

on their 'own ground', and unless there is considerable deterioration in the meantime they have players to entertain as well as to be effective. With a player like Cruyff, who seems to be about the most talked-about player in the world as I write, and whose idol, not surprisingly, was the indefatigable di Stefano, the Dutch have made enormous strides without boring people silly by playing nine full-backs.

I hope an adventurous team, encouraging the individual, wins it because footballers as a race are great copiers, and the game as a spectacle will be the better for it.

As for me, I hope to spend the rest of my life trying to repay football for what it has done for me. If I could sum up the lessons it has taught me, they are not to open my mouth too wide or I shall certainly put my foot in it; respond to warmth with warmth and encourage it if yours needs to be the first move; and in management, be not remote, but give respect and, even more important, give affection, if you expect to receive it.

Without affection we might win something today but in the end will have gained nothing.

A Selection of Crime Thrillers from Sphere

All Sphere Books are available at your bookshop or
newsagent, or can be ordered from the following address:

Sphere Books, Cash Sales Department,
P.O. Box 11, Falmouth, Cornwall.

Please send cheque or postal order (no currency), and allow
7p per copy to cover the cost of postage and packing
in U.K. or overseas.